A Special Collectors' Preview Edition
Featuring
The Most Comprehensive
Sonny Boy Williamson II Discography

'FESSOR MOJO'S "DON'T START ME TO TALKIN"

William E. Donoghue

©*Mojo Visions Productions, Inc.*
A portion of the revenues from this book will be donated to BluesAid

Published by
MOJO Visions
a division of
Elliott & James Publishing
P.O. Box 19535
Seattle, WA 98109

Copyright 1997 by William E. Donoghue
All rights reserved

ISBN: 0-9637899-5-3

Manufactured in the United States
10 9 8 7 6 5 4 3 2

No part of this book may be reproduced, stored in or introduced into a retrieval system, or transmitted, in any form or by any means (electronic, mechanical, photocopying, recording or otherwise) without the prior written permission of the publisher.

Supervising Editor: Luke Dawson
Cover Design: Shael Anderson
Desktop Publisher: Shael Anderson

Table of Contents

Acknowledgments	5
Preface	9
Mystery #1	11
Sonny Boy's Story	15
Mystery #2	20
Mystery #3	20
Mystery #4	20
Mystery #5	23
Mystery #6	27
Mystery #7	28
Mystery #8	58
Mystery #9	63
Mystery #10	64
Discography	67

Acknowledgments

First, I would like to thank Stevenson Palfi, producer of "Piano Players Rarely Ever Play Together," the award-winning documentary on 'Fessor Longhair, Tuts Washington and Allen Toussaint for his encouragement and inspiration. It was he who first nicknamed me "'Fessor Mojo" and it was on one of his Allen Toussaint/JazzFest shoots that I gained my first working video documentary experience.

I would like to give special thanks to three people who started me on this quest for Sonny Boy Williamson II; Jim O'Neal, founder of Rooster Blues Records and co-founder of *Living Blues* magazine, who first introduced me to the other two, Sonny Boy's sisters Julia Barner and Mary Ashford. I would also like to thank the elusive Betty Peaques, Sonny Boy's niece, who first invited me to write a biography of her Uncle Sonny and then disappeared back into the Delta; Joe Vinikow, primary cinematographer of the project; Jim Kelton, my creative researcher and screenwriter; Annique Bennett, who started the project with me; Karla Kombrink, my director of public relations without whom many of the contacts might not have been made; Rob Fabroni, sound track producer of "The Last Waltz"

'Fessor Mojo's "Don't Start Me To Talkin"

movie; Bob Koester, who generously provided us interview space at the Jazz Record Mart; John Ruskey of the Delta Blues Museum who invited me to conduct my first blues seminar at the Sunflower Blues Festival; Synthia Edwards of the Delta Cultural Center; Judy Peiser of the Center For The Study of Southern Folklore, Tater Red, Denise Tapp and Sharon Corbett whose insights have been especially helpful; the interview subjects listed below and my Seattle WA and Milford MA staffs who have been patient with me as I pursued this irresistible muse and who eventually became Sonny Boy Williamson blues converts.

I have interviewed on video **Lillian McMurry** (who discovered and recorded Sonny Boy Williamson and Elmore James for her pioneering and well-respected Trumpet Records label in Jackson MS), **Gayle Dean Wardlow**, (who discovered Robert Johnson's death certificate in 1968 and recently discovered the hidden note on its reverse)., **Dick Waterman**, (who rediscovered and/or managed Son House, Skip James, Mississippi John Hurt and Junior Wells), **Z. L. Hill** ("Mama" to her guests, proprietor of the legendary Riverside Hotel, Home of the Delta Blues), **Sam Carr** and **Frank Frost** (Sonny Boy's working backup band from 1956-65), **"Sunshine" Sonny Payne** (King Biscuit Time's long-time host on and off since 1942), **Jim O'Neal** (co-founder of *Living Blues*, owner of Rooster Blues Records, and blues oral historian extraordinaire); **Morris Gist** (owner of Sonny Boy's apartment building and owner/operator of Gist's Music in Helena AK), **Bubba Sullivan** (founder of the Sonny Boy Blues Society and BluesAid), **David "Honeyboy" Edwards** (Delta bluesman/hobo and friend of Sonny Boy since 1929, as well as sole surviving member of the band which played at Three Forks the night

Acknowledgments

Robert Johnson was poisoned), **Bob Koester** (founder of Delmark records, who, along with his artist Sleepy John Estes, accompanied Sonny Boy to Europe for the 1964 American Folk Blues Festival), **Chris Strachwitz** (founder of Arhoolie Records, who was on the 1964 American Folk Blues Festival tour with Lightnin' Hopkins and who visited with and photographed Sonny Boy in Helena AR in May 1965, a few weeks before Sonny Boy's death), **Junior Wells** (who had a memorable and life changing encounter with Rice Miller in a cotton field in the late '40s), **Mighty Joe Young** & **Billy Boy Arnold** (big fans of John Lee Williamson who told us of Rice Miller's cool reception in Chicago), **Dick Shurman** (blues writer who told us a classic story about Rice Miller, his bottle and his pig's ear sandwich) and **Charlie Musselwhite** (outstanding Mississippi blues harpist who told us what was in Sonny Boy's ubiquitous briefcase).

In addition, I have had extensive phone and personal interviews with **Julia Barner** and **Mary Ashford** (Rice Miller's /Sonny Boy's sisters), **Mark Hoffman** & **Jim Segrist** (erstwhile Howlin' Wolf biographers) **Ed Komara** (Blues Archives, Ole Miss) and **Peter Lee** (former *Living Blues* editor, Sonny Boy researcher, and Delta record producer/label owner).

It has indeed been a memorable search for the "real" person behind the wonderful music of Sonny Boy Williamson II.

                William E. "'Fessor Mojo" Donoghue
                Seattle WA
                September 1996

'Fessor Mojo's "Don't Start Me To Talkin"

Preface

Many famous blues artists lie in unmarked graves. Few have even the simple tombstones found in most cemeteries. The simple reason is that the family is often more willing to expend their meager resources on a funeral for the living than a marker for the dead. Sonny Boy Williamson II is buried near the edge of the woods in a well-kept grave marked with an elegant tombstone in Whitfield Cemetery on a peaceful country road in Tutwiler MS. Coins, harps, guitar picks and other tributes left by his many fans are found at its base.

Sonny Boy Williamson II's elegant tombstone was respectfully placed by Trumpet Records' owner Lillian McMurry in 1980. Its inscription is based on information supplied by Mattie Williamson Thurmon, Sonny Boy's widow, and Julia Barner, Sonny Boy's sister and it reads:

ALECK MILLER
BETTER KNOWN AS
WILLIE "SONNY BOY" WILLIAMSON
BORN MAR. 11, 1905
DIED JUNE 23, 1965

SON OF
JIM MILLER AND MILLIE MILLER

INTERNATIONALLY FAMOUS HARMONICA AND VOCAL BLUES ARTIST DISCOVERED AND RECORDED BY TRUMPET RECORDS, JACKSON MISS. FROM 1950 TO 1955

'Fessor Mojo's "Don't Start Me To Talkin'"

In spite of its good intentions, the inscription exemplifies the mysteries surrounding this enigmatic bluesman. The true details of his identity are lost in the mysteries of the Mississippi Delta, where multiple names, vague and "overlooked" life histories, "outside" children, "blues names" better remembered than birth names, and hidden or forgotten pasts are the legacy of the history which gave birth to the blues.

In detail, the inscription is not even close. In fact, his name was probably *Alex* Miller. He was best known among blacks by his nickname, *"Rice"* Miller. "Willie" is apparently his *brother's* name. His real surname is *not* Williamson, it is either "Miller" (his stepfather's name), "Ford" (his mother's surname); or, if he was an "outside" child, his unknown father's name. He was probably born *either* around the turn of the century or shortly after 1910. The early possible dates are 1897 (as he claimed in his 1963 song, "The Story of Sonny Boy Williamson"), 1899 or 1901.

"The bluesman with the photographic memory", Honeyboy Edwards, when asked "When did you first meet Sonny Boy?" answered "In 1929, I was 14 and he was 28." Hence 1901, which he also told Blues Unlimited in 1963, was possibly his birth year.

The other possible birth time was around 1911. (Sonny Boy was apparently not listed in the 1910 census. It would also preclude the April 7, 1909 date that he claimed on his passport.)

Finally, the easiest thing to get right is also wrong. He died on May 25, 1965 (according to his death certificate).

Preface

Lillian McMurry, who paid for the elegant burial marker told us: *"I did not know that he had any other name except Willie 'Sonny Boy' Williamson until after he was dead. Then I kept hearing people refer to him as 'Rice' Miller. I finally got the truth outta Mattie [Sonny Boy's widow] and Sonny Boy's sister, Julia Barner, at the time that I was getting the tombstone made. And that was when I learned that he was actually Aleck Miller."*

Sonny Boy Mystery #1 — <u>When was Sonny Boy Williamson II ("Rice" Miller) born?</u> Frankly, this a tough one to solve. Some research into the 1910, 1920 and 1930 census records might unearth some clues to this mystery. It certainly would make it a bit easier for us to write his biography, since it would give us some clues as to his age when he experienced the events of his life. Maybe someone will come up with more definitive proof of his birthdate than the several dates given by his family. More details of his family's names, birth sequence, and their birthdates might shed some light on this mystery. If you beat us to discovering the solution to this mystery, we would certainly appreciate your help. I would also be curious to find out about his brother "Willie," whose name Sonny Boy used.

Rice Miller AKA Sonny Boy Williamson II was the essence of the Delta bluesman, emerging to make his brilliant music, keeping on the move to avoid unnecessary interaction with the law, and then reappearing under a different name in a different city; a classic man of mystery. We may never know his real birthdate and, therefore, we will never know his real age. But we can know much about the man and we are discovering more and more as we continue our search.

What you have in your hands is the first publication of the most extensive oral history research ever conducted into the life, the world and the recordings of Aleck or Alex "Rice" Miller AKA Sonny Boy Williamson II. It includes the most comprehensive discography to date and it starts with a collectors' preview of the contents of "Don't Start Me To Talkin," a forthcoming book and video documentary of the mysterious world of Sonny Boy Williamson II.

It is possible in the coming years you will see a Sonny Boy Williamson Box set, tribute album and/or concert, and possibly a dramatic movie or TV show. It all depends on where Sonny Boy's story takes us and who chooses to join us on our journey.

BE AN OFFICIAL "MOJO VISIONS BLUES DETECTIVE" ($US100 Reward)

For now, there is "Don't Start Me Talkin'", however, this is a continuously developing blues documentary project and we invite you to provide us with your Sonny Boy Williamson II stories, feelings and input. As we progress, you will see a number of Sonny Boy Mysteries in Boxes throughout the text. If you have a story which you think could explain these mysteries, see the end of the preview, just before the discography, for directions on how to contact us and help us tell the full story.

PREFACE

> A $US100 reward, a possible personal appearance in the video, and published public recognition in the "official" edition of this book will be provided for the first person to provide us with the lead to the solution of any of these Sonny Boy mysteries. "Mojo Visions Blues Detective" T-shirts will be awarded to all who are first to either solve the numbered mysteries or provide us with verifiable Sonny Boy stories we can use in the documentary. All submissions become the property of Mojo Visions. Offer expires June 30, 1997. Employees and consultants to Mojo Visions Productions and affiliated companies are not eligible.

Now, allow me to introduce you to the man of the hour, Sonny Boy Williamson II, and the genesis our quest.

'Fessor Mojo's "Don't Start Me To Talkin"

Sonny Boy Williamson II

"The old rascal is on the loose again."

Introduction: How Rice Miller Started To Talkin' To Me

On the hot, lazy Delta afternoon of August 12, 1995, guided by Jim O'Neal, co-founder of *Living Blues* magazine, I visited the homes of two charming elderly ladies: Julia Barner, 95 (Born August 8, 1900), and Mary Ashford, 89 (Born May 1, 1906), the last two of Sonny Boy Williamson II's 20 siblings ("All by the same parents," they claimed). That chance meeting started me on what I can only call a "quest," a search for knowledge, in the grandest sense.

At the time, I was only aware of Sonny Boy Williamson's fascinating music, through songs like "Eyesight To The Blind," which I knew was included, as the only song not written by a band member, in the rock opera "Tommy". I remember encountering as a young man, records of his intriguing "Your Funeral and My Trial" and "Fattenin' Frogs For Snakes", two memorable blues poems which stuck firmly in my mind. I knew little of Sonny Boy Williamson as a person, except that his real name was rumored to be "Rice" Miller. I also knew about John Lee "Sonny Boy" Williamson, who was the first to record using the name "Sonny Boy Williamson," and thus Miller was often refered to as Sonny Boy Williamson II or "the second Sonny Boy Williamson." At the time, while I knew the basic facts about him, I only knew him through his wonderful Chess records. I had never even seen a Trumpet record until recently. I had started buying Sonny Boy's Chess blues records at my local record store in West Chester PA, in the mid-fifties.

I was soon to learn that few people, if any, had *ever really* known knew him as a person as well as they thought. I have found no one who knew him well in all his many contexts; the Delta, in prison, in Chicago, in Europe, in the studio, at home, on the road and in the jukes.

In separate and brief hour-long visits with each sister, they introduced me to the world of the young Alex Miller, known to his family as "Rice" or "Sonny". Julia Barner acted out for me conversations she had with her younger brother "Rice" Miller when he was a child. "I needs money to get some new shoes," he would whine, "You gots a quarter and you gots a dime. I needs some new shoes. I'll pay you back. I gots money comin' to me." "Sonny, you're not going to pay it back. I know that," she would say to him as if he were there in the room. She called him "Sonny" (not "Sonny Boy," but you begin to understand his partial rationale for his claim to being "the original Sonny Boy")

According to her funeral program, she was born in 1900. If that is accurate, if Sonny Boy was her younger brother he was probably born *after* 1900.

In the process I was learning quickly, under Jim O'Neal's tutelage, the need to confirm "facts" independently in the mercurial world of the Delta and oral blues history. "Facts" are remembered vaguely and conveniently, years and months and dates are floating "truths" without anchors, and the isolation from national media and other peoples' history strained through the filter of poverty and illiteracy creates a whole new reality.

The special challenges of collecting oral blues history are in a world I was to discover had been largely overlooked in the literature of the blues. Thank God for *Living Blues* magazine which for years filled the void in the recorded literature. Without music magazines and liner notes, there would be precious little knowledge of the world of the blues.

Indeed, blues history seemed to be a world in which some wanted to "whitewash" history for their own purposes or cover up and simplify before they even knew what they were covering up. At best, it was a world which most researchers insisted Sonny Boy's story was to remain unknown and one which he himself was reluctant to discuss. One writer, apparently attempting to protect his "right" to Sonny Boy's secrets, even "warned" others not to explore the subject.

My motivation was simple. I found "Rice" Miller's life story fascinating. To really know him and his impact on the world of music, I needed to talk to the people who knew him first hand and who his music had touched. "Rice" Miller's story is special because it encompasses the entire history of the blues, it includes both the Pre-War and Post-War blues periods, the country blues and the Rhythm and

Blues golden eras, and it was the story of a man who juggled several lives in the process. Very simply, "Rice" Miller's story is the essence of the blues experience.

But as happened during the production of "Piano Players Rarely Ever Play Together," my friend Stevenson Palfi's outstanding documentary which was abruptly interrupted by the death of 'Fessor Longhair, my journey was also to be touched by the deaths of Sonny Boy's irreplaceable sisters Julia Barner and Mary Ashford.

THE TRAGEDY

On October 11, 1995, barely two months after I had interviewed them, both sisters tragically perished together in a late night house fire. A benefit was held in November featuring James Cotton, Sonny Boy's one-time protégé, which raised about half the cost of their burial. I found out about their deaths when a niece of Sonny Boy's, Betty Peaques, who I had met at her aunts' homes, called me in December with the news that they had died so tragically. I was touched with the great loss of these wonderful ladies and their living link to Sonny Boy's story.

Later, I decided to provide the remaining half of the cost of the ladies' burial. I felt that it was the least I could do considering how generous they had been sharing with me their very open reminiscences of Sonny Boy, which lead me to the fascinating story you are reading. Indeed, still later, I helped found BluesAid, a charity which would assist elderly bluesmen in their later years and assure a burial with dignity in appreciation for their musical legacy to us all. I am not seeking credit for my generosity; I am only seeking to help you understand why part of the proceeds of this book are being contributed to BluesAid. It is a project to which I am committed and one which I encourage you to support..

The sisters are currently buried in an unmarked grave (which demands a tombstone) in Whitfield Cemetery near Sonny Boy Williamson II ("Rice" Miller) whose tombstone presides over not a mound in the earth but an indentation. Is it possible the old rascal is on the loose again? I would not put it past him.

THE BOOK RESEARCH PROJECT IS BORN

Betty Peaques, Sonny Boy's niece, asked if I would be interested in writing a book about her "Uncle Sonny Boy". I am a successful author in my own field with my own publishing company. But this was my first foray into writing books on the blues. I was not sure how to go about responsibly and credibly researching such a book! I told her I would think about it. As I started consulting the many volumes in my extensive roots music history and criticism (a lifetime fascination with me) library, I discovered many entries about Sonny Boy Williamson. He was universally-acknowledged to be a very important and influential bluesman. However, most of the articles simply rehashed the very few, often inconsistent and (as I would soon discover) inaccurate "facts" about Sonny Boy. Everyone, it seemed, loved and respected his music. Few, if any, actually knew much about his life. This story was getting interesting.

It was then that I decided that the only way to "find" the real Sonny Boy Williamson was to talk with those who loved him; his family, his friends and his fans. As the interviews progressed, my assumptions about Sonny Boy's importance were confirmed by such people as Lillian McMurry (of the legendary Trumpet Records), Bob Koester (of Delmark Records), Bruce Iglauer (of Alligator Records), Chris Strachwitz (of Arhoolie Records), and blues harpists Charlie Musselwhite, Junior Wells, Billy Branch, and Levon Helm. Of all the blues artists, Sonny Boy Williamson II was their favorite. And in the case of the harpists, he was a source of great inspiration. Even Sonny Boy I worshiper, Billy Boy Arnold, told me how important Sonny Boy II was to the world of the blues.

I was on to something.

FLASH AHEAD ONE YEAR

On August 2nd, 1996, a year minus ten days later, I presented a seminar at The Delta Blues Museum in Clarksdale MS on The Life of Sonny Boy Williamson II ("Rice" Miller), as part of the annual Sunflower Blues Festival. Unbeknownst to me at the time, the tiny audience for my simple presentation included some of the most knowledgeable blues researchers and writers in the world.

As the climax of my introduction to Sonny Boy, I presented the man himself via a video of his 1964 performance in England at the American Folk Blues Festival's "I Hear The Blues" Grenada TV Special. It was a very touching moment.

I was startled by the response. As Sonny Boy's gently rocking harp rhythms filled the room and introduced "Keep It To Yourself," *the entire museum,* including many people who were only perusing the museum's exhibits, *went strangely silent and began gravitating toward his image.* Sonny Payne, long-time host of Sonny Boy's "King Biscuit Time" radio show, and Sam Carr and Frank Frost, Sonny Boy's late '50s Delta rhythm section, *looked as if they had seen a ghost.* It was only then that I began to fully appreciate the magic, the genius and the charisma of this man. I could understand why King Biscuit Time was and is such a special radio event.

Two months later, at the 1996 King Biscuit Blues Festival, held virtually in Sonny Boy's backyard, I repeated the seminar to a much larger crowd.

SONNY BOY WAS BOTH CHARISMATIC AND THREATENING

Sonny Boy was not the kind of man who even his best friends could ever get close to. He was a BIG man; reportedly over 6' 5", 230-250 lb., with size 14 shoes. He would often slit the sides of his shoes in order to gain enough room for his huge feet, at least until he apparently found out where to buy or have custom-made boots in the larger sizes he needed. He drank steadily and heavily (a lifelong diet of as much as three to four bottles of 100 proof Old Grand Dad, Johnny Walker or Ancient Age whiskey a day). His briefcase held his bottle, his cigarettes, a brace of harps in all keys and a hatchet (which allegedly he knew how to hurl accurately from across a room). His pocket invariably contained a switchblade knife (which he was reputed to be able to extract from his pocket fully-extended). Even his closest associates respected and feared him. He could hold a grudge for a long time. As you might expect of a lonely musician, he had a reputation for fighting and womanizing.

Sonny Boy could be a courtly and well-dressed dandy. As early as 1937, he was appearing in a snappy custom-made (?) English-style double-breasted wool jacket and stylish bowler hat (a derby). When he finally got to England in 1963-65, he had several suits made, including the legendary two-colored suit with alternating blue and gray panels on both jacket and pants.

Gayle Dean Wardlow tells of a Hattiesburg MS pianist from the '20s and '30s named Cooney Vaughn, who recorded with the Mississippi Juke Band, who was 6' 4" or 6' 5" with a goatee and was known to wear a derby who might have been Sonny Boy's sartorial inspiration. He was an early influence of Little Brother Montgomery who recorded "Cooney Vaughn's Tremblin' Blues."

He could also be cautiously generous. He would buy strangers drinks, take on young protégés and accompanists (like James Cotton at age 6, Frank Frost and Robert Jr. Lockwood in his early 'teens.), lend money to friends (on the firm premise that it would always be repaid on time - you can understand his desire to have at least something he could count on in a world where promises were rarely kept, especially by record companies) and, after gambling his band's money away the night before, he would go out on the street in the morning and earn it back in short order. He was known to accompany a friends on their records, as he did for Tampa Red, Baby Boy Warren, Peck Curtis, Dudlow Taylor and even Josh White.

Musically, on the other hand, he was "King of the Harmonica" (as he was introduced by Memphis Slim and

"Sunshine" Sonny Payne). The cry of his blues harp (like the rocking beat of a churning Zydeco accordion) could be the late night sob of the blues or the clarion call to "party down." Sonny Boy was a virtuoso harpist. He could coax as many as five keys out of the cheap blues "harps" (Hohner Marine Band harmonicas) he preferred. Each harp is designed to play in a single key. He could play a tiny harp inside his mouth, play one harp with his mouth while playing a second with his nose and hold a harp in his mouth like a cigar while playing in tune and decidedly on the beat. He could and would jam with anyone. He recorded with Rahsaan Roland Kirk in Copenhagen in 1963, he jammed with Dexter Gordon in Milan and, on tour in Germany, he was known to jam with the violinist at a local restaurant. No matter what or how he played, his rocking rhythms and choppy riffs were irresistible.

SONNY BOY WAS AN ESCAPED CONVICT

Aleck "Rice" Miller AKA Sonny Boy Williamson II, if you insist, although he would insist he was "Mr. Original Sonny Boy Williamson", (as he introduced himself to saxman Archie Shepp in Copenhagen in 1963) was an escaped convict who became an international blues star under another man's name. Read that amazing claim once again, for you, if you are white, are among the first to discover his lifelong secret. If you are black and lived in the Delta, this is probably no surprise to you.

Lillian McMurry, of Trumpet Records (1950-1955), was the first to record Sonny Boy Williamson II and the last, it seems, to know his real name. On the occasion of designing a grave marker in 1980, fifteen years after his demise, she discovered the real name of her old friend.

Lillian McMurry, of course, knew that he was not the Sonny Boy Williamson I who recorded "Good Morning Little School Girl" in 1937, and who had died in a gambling dispute in Chicago in 1948. But "Sonny Boy" was not an uncommon name for a black man in the South. So she accepted him at his word. To further perpetuate the myth of his identity, Sonny Boy had married Mattie Gordon in 1949 using the name Willie "Sonny Boy" Williamson. His insistence that he was "The Original Sonny Boy, the Only Sonny Boy" was backed by the claim that his father's last name was Williamson, a misrepresentation that went so far as to be perpetuated by his widow on his death certificate.

Aleck "Rice" Miller (his sister Julia "Shug" Barner, said that he liked rice so much they named him for it) was born sometime around the turn of the century (1894, 1897, 1899 and 1901 are frequently mentioned birthdates; he tended to prefer December 5, 1897 which he claimed in a late recording) the twenty-first child of Millie Ford and Jim Miller in Glendora, Tallahatchie County, Mississippi. He grew up in Tutwiler, and also in Tallahatchie County, Mississippi, where his Pentecostal family was delighted to see him very early on, (allegedly at the age of six), adopt the name (his first of many names) "Reverend Blue". He traveled around the Delta playing church music at courthouses, schools and street corners and at churches, picnics, barbecues... wherever he could play, draw a crowd and earn tips.

Sonny Boy seems to have traveled all over the Delta with his harmonica (and sometimes with a guitar). At one point he taught Howlin' Wolf (Chester Burnett, ironically and propitiously himself Howlin' Wolf II, as J. T. "Funny Papa" Smith had already recorded "Howlin' Wolf Blues" in the 1920s) the fundamentals of the harmonica. Later he would marry Howlin' Wolf's half-sister Mary (according to Wolf in *Living Blues* Vol. 1 #1) or possibly Marget (according to Mary Ashford, one of Rice's older sisters talking to Gayle Dean Wardlow) or maybe no one (Wolf's family allegedly doesn't seem to remember a half-sister Mary).

At this time, I can only assume that he made the same discovery that B. B. King made on Beale Street in Memphis: sing church songs and you will get a lot of "amens" and compliments, sing the blues and the tips begin to flow.

Certainly it was not just playing the blues which would shape his life at this point. Two events apparently changed his life in the late 1920s or early 1930s; (1) he would have a violent dispute with his father forcing him to leave home. Ironically his father died soon after in 1929, and his family could not find Sonny Boy to tell him about the funeral (again according to Mary Ashford's 1972 conversations with Gayle Dean Wardlow) and (2) sometime in probably 1930 or 1938 (according to Sonny Boy when talking about the "mistake" he referred to in 1957's "Fattenin' Frogs For Snakes" something ominous and life changing occurred.

Four possible explanations are offered for the event which would qualify as his ominous "mistake," (1) he stole a neighbor's mule, painted it white and when the rains washed it clean he was arrested and sent to Parchman Farm, the Mississippi State Penitentiary, from which he was allegedly allowed to escape (according to Julia Barner, Sonny

Boy's favorite when explaining Sonny Boy's hiding his real name from Lillian McMurry), (2) the violent argument with his father reported in "Blues Who's Who", (3) in 1936 he allegedly hung a white man's mule in anger (Sonny Boy confided this dark secret to his friends) and (4) the very real possibility that Sonny Boy Williamson either accompanied Robert Johnson or was taken by Robert Johnson to some "crossroads" experience where Sonny Boy may have also "sold his soul to the devil".

At this point all or some of these explanations are possible or probable. Jim O'Neal, founder of *Living Blues* Magazine, once wrote that in collecting oral blues history "things are not always as they appear to be." That very insight is at the heart of my fascination with this story.

You see, to oversimplify the situation and, at to risk my being politically incorrect, whites assumed that black slaves who did not speak their language or understand English had no culture. The opposite is obviously true; black Africans had a very rich culture. In fact, Africans had music and literature when the Europeans were still living in caves. The insistence of white slaveowners on denying that black slaves were capable of having a sophisticated culture resulted in that culture being suppressed. History tells us they did, however, forbid Blacks to use the talking drums, indeed drums of any kind, for fear they could communicate to organize resistance.

It was the existence of that very rich culture and its heavy suppression that created the need among blacks to communicate and express it. The blues, and what was then referred to by whites as "the gospel blues", was the medium for coded communications between blacks. Most whites never did get the coded information in the blues. A black worker would sing to his mule what he wanted to say to his master, for example.

Looking back, the richness of this suppressed African culture is what ultimately the crucible which gave the blues an important but overlooked function. Whites' often assumed that there was nothing of consequence in black culture and did not listen closely to the blues' lyrics. Blacks used that very oversight as an opportunity to metaphorically say things to whites in song they could not or would not say to a white face. For example, a frustrated and angry field worker could cuss out his mule in song instead of his master. Sonny Boy could sing to dishonest but naive promoters that he would not be "Fattenin' any more frogs for snakes."

Two poignant examples of the cultural barriers were provided by Trumpet Records' Lillian McMurry.

(1) The effectiveness of Sonny Boy's desire for his privacy is pointed up by the fact that Sonny Boy's real name was kept from Mrs. McMurry until fifteen years after his death, and then it was revealed only when she was asking his sisters' help in placing a tombstone on his grave.

(2) The fact that she chuckles today having recently discovered that an apparent "four-day creep" to which Sonny Boy refers in "Too Close Together" (a song about his amorous relations with two sisters who lived, you got it, too close together) was, in reality, a "fore-day creep" or an early morning visit to a (usually married) lover's bed. That's a whole different meaning than "a long slow journey."

Even Mrs. McMurry, an astute, experienced and respectful recorder of the best of the black culture overlooked the subtly racy content. She knew well that subtle racy content could keep an otherwise successful record from being played. Watch for the coded information in the blues and it can open up a fuller understanding of the Southern culture.

SONNY BOY WILLIAMSON WAS A MAN IN TURMOIL

Sonny Boy Williamson was an escaped convict most of his adult life. Given the fact that black men were often jailed at harvest time to assure an adequate supply of workers on nearby plantations, and other facts of life in the Delta, it would be safe to suspect that any black leaving the Delta was regarded an escaped convict. But Sonny Boy was apparently allowed to escape, and the thought of being sent back to the prison fields was frightening to him.

Allegedly, in his teens he wanted to go to town to jam with other bluesmen or play for nickels and dimes on the corner — so he stole a neighbor's mule. As a clumsy disguise, he painted the mule white with whitewash. When the rains came, as you might expect, he was busted.

Back then, punishment for blacks had to be swift and certain. He was apparently arrested, tried and sentenced to Parchman Farm, the Mississippi State Penitentiary, virtually in his backyard of Tutwiler MS. For a self-centered, independent, free-thinking and, even more, outspoken man like Rice Miller, this was a disastrous place to be. As if prison life and the dreaded hard farm work were not punishment enough, those conditions were compounded by the fact that he had become a musician to avoid that hard and arduous life. The loss of his independent lifestyle, added to his being subjected to people with arbitrary life and death authority over him, must have terrified him.

God knows what happened to him in Parchman farm. All we seem to "know" is that his harmonica playing apparently charmed a guard who allowed him to escape. That story sounds like wishful thinking. More than likely, they allowed him to escape simply because he was not a good worker and they didn't want the cost of feeding him.

It was after his escape that his practice of hiding behind different names in different towns began to emerge. As a child, he apparently used the name "Reverend Blue" when he played church music around the Delta. But after his escape, he was careful not to use his prison name, "Rice" Miller for fear of being discovered. He preferred to inhabit the night world of the jukes where his past would not be revealed.

He began to call himself "Harmonica-blowin' Slim" in the Delta, where Jessie Mae Hemphill's family remembers him as "Slim". In 1937, he was "Little Boy Blue" on Eldorado IL's WEBQ radio station and, by late 1938, he began to appear was "Sonny Boy Williamson" in Helena AR.

One astute blues observer speculates that he could have discovered on his first radio show, WEBQ [His circa 1937 flyer for the show claimed he appeared five times a week on Mondays (twice), Wednesdays, Thursdays and Fridays.] that he could be anyone. Considering that he may have just recently been in prison or might soon be in prison around this time, you could understand his need to masquerade under a different name.

'Fessor Mojo's "Don't Start Me To Talkin"

Sonny Boy Mystery # 2—The Inside Story of the WEBQ "Little Boy Blue" Radio Show. When exactly did Sonny Boy have his radio show on WEBQ? What was the format? Why did it stop airing? Who was the sponsor? How did he get the show? What was he doing in Eldorado IL? Are there any photos or artifacts beyond the flier for the show? What was the 25 cents price mentioned on the flier for? his personal appearances?

Sonny Boy Mystery #3 & #4—Evidence of Sonny Boy's Possible Prison Sentences in 1930 (?) and 1938 (?) and (?). In 1957 Sonny Boy made a recording of "Fattenin' Frogs For Snakes" in which he referred to his "Downfall back in nineteen and thirty" (he also said 1938 in most other versions). Is he referring to a prison term or terms? What were the crimes? Stealing the mule he painted white? If you accept the later birth date 1911 and the story that it was in his teens, he was nineteen in 1930. If you note the gap in his life story around 1938, that could be another possibility? According to my sources, "he hung a white man's mule" in 1936 for which he could have been sentenced. How do you get to "correct all of [your] mistakes" in 1957? What kind of "mistakes" can you correct? Or is it just a song?

Clues *may* be found in his song, "Fattenin' Frogs For Snakes";

> "It took me a long time to find out my mistake
> It took me a long time, a long time, to find out my mistake.
> It sure did, man
> But I'll bet you my bottom dollar
> I'm not fattenin' no more frogs for snakes.
>
> "I found out my downfall back in nineteen and thirty (I started checkin')
> I found out my downfall from nineteen and thirty
> I'm tellin' all my friends,
> I'm not fattening no more frogs for snakes
> (Alright Now!)
>
> "Till nineteen and fifty-seven I got to correct all my mistakes
> Oh man, nineteen and fifty-seven I got to correct all my mistakes
> I'm telling my friends including my wife and everybody else
> I'm not fattening no more frogs for snakes."
>
> "Fattenin' Frogs For Snakes"...Sonny Boy Williamson (1957)

    He was a different person in each city. Think about it. At various times he was allegedly known as Aleck (or Alex) "Rice" Miller, "Reverend Blue", "Harmonica-Blowin' Slim" in the Delta, "Little Boy Blue" in Eldorado IL, Willie Williams in Helena AR, Willie Miller (designed to be confused with his brother), Willie "Sonny Boy" Williamson (on his contract with Trumpet Records, on his marriage certificate, and on his tombstone), Sonny Boy

Williamson, "Biscuit" Miller, "Flour" Miller", or even "Sonny Boy" Williams (on a Chicago Elmore James poster and on his passport), and, in Europe, Sonny Boy Williamson II. His close friends even called him "Footsie" (due to his habit of slitting the sides of his shoes for comfort), and "The Goat" (apparently due to his goatee).

Does this sound like a man hiding from something? But we are getting ahead of our story.

"RICE" MILLER IN THE EARLY THIRTIES

"Rice" Miller, born in Glendora (Tallahatchie county) MS grew up the youngest of 21 children of a Pentecostal family in Tutwiler (also in Tallahatchie county) MS. His step-(?)father, Jim Miller was a blacksmith, as close to an independent businessman as a black could be in the pre-integration Delta. His children all had nicknames "Shug", "Dog", "Cat", and of course, "Rice" among them.

Allegedly, he learned to play harp (harmonica) at an early age (six?) and he soon adopted the name "Reverend Blue" and played picnics, church meetings, etc. for tips. It is rumored that he only played church music as a child. At some point he added the blues to his repertoire. If he was, indeed, a serious church goer, this transition from God's music to the devil's music was not to be taken lightly.

In the late 1920's he reportedly had a violent fight with his father resulting in his leaving home. Once again, the transition from a young churchgoing man to a bluesman would have to have been traumatic.

> **Sonny Boy Mystery #5 — "Rice" Miller's Early Life**—What can you tell us about "Rice" Miller's early life? What was the dispute about with his father, was it his lack of interest in sharecropping and picking cotton or something more closely related to his lifestyle? What was Rice's involvement in the church? What was the transition from church music to the blues all about? Was it important to Rice?

SONNY BOY MEETS ROBERT JOHNSON

The beginning years of the 1930s probably were traumatic years for both Rice Miller and Robert Johnson. First, it was the beginning of the Depression and there was certainly no special dispensation given to the Delta during the Depression. When the Depression hit, it hit hard.

Rice Miller had left his very supportive home (I am sure his sisters Julia and Mary among them, doted on him. He should have lived a comfortable life.). Suddenly, he was on the road hoboing and singing the blues.

Robert Johnson had his problems in the early 1930s as well. In 1929, his wife had died in childbirth resulting in his fledgling family being wiped out. The town, Tunica, ostracized him for the terrible thing he had done to his wife, "their little girl"; he had been ramblin' on the road leaving her alone to die. Robert was initially not a very good guitar player. He was then primarily known for his harp playing and it was only when he got "lost" somewhere and returned a brilliant guitarist (according to Son House's stories of throwing him out for playing his guitar

'Fessor Mojo's "Don't Start Me To Talkin"

so badly one year and being very impressed when he encountered him again a few years later).

One can only speculate when these two ramblin' blues men met but they share a life full of "crossroads" experiences at similar times. By 1936, apparently they were friends. Certainly in 1934 Rice Miller knew Robert Jr. Lockwood's family in Marvell AR, as he was bugging him to travel with him as his accompanist. At some point in the early 1930s, Robert Johnson met Robert Jr.'s mother, Estella Coleman and Robert Johnson taught Robert Lockwood Jr. how to play guitar. Thereafter, Robert Lockwood Jr. would be called "Robert Jr." Lockwood after Johnson.

On August 13, 1938, Robert Johnson was playing at Three Forks country store outside of Greenwood MS. I discussed that night with Honeyboy Edwards. Apparently, about midnight, Johnson was given some poisoned whiskey and could not play his final set. Soon after, Honeyboy Edwards says he arrived at Three Forks and that Rice Miller/Sonny Boy Williamson arrived shortly afterward. As Johnson lay on a bed in the back room, Honeyboy, Sonny Boy and Tommy McClennan would jam the night away.

The three had been playing this gig for several months and Robert Johnson had been keeping time with a married woman quite openly. Apparently someone, the woman or her father, poisoned Robert Johnson's moonshine whiskey. It was Sonny Boy who told Johnny Shines that Robert Johnson died three days later in a private home in Baptist Town, a section of Greenwood MS. Gayle Dean Wardlow has recently uncovered the reverse side of Robert Johnson's death certificate which indicates that Robert Johnson died on a plantation. He had no doctor because Johnson did not work for the plantation owner. This new information is consistent with Honeyboy's story that he did not see Robert Johnson on the day he died but possibly not Sonny Boy's. Sonny Boy claimed that Robert Johnson died in his arms or at least that is what he told Levon Helm in 1965. He told a different story to Neil Slaven in 1963. The two stories are differ but may be reconcilable.

Sonny Boy Williamson told Levon Helm, Marvell AR-born drummer, of The Band shortly before he died in 1965 that he was there when Johnson. "While we waited, someone asked Sonny Boy whether he's known Robert Johnson." Helm writes "Knew him!" Sonny Boy asked incredulously "Boy, Robert Johnson died in my arms.." (Source: This Wheel's On Fire: Levon Helm and the Story of The Band, Levon Helm with Stephen Davis.)

That story is consistent with what Sonny Boy apparently told Johnny Shines who quoted Sonny Boy as the source of his information in the John Hammond video "The Search For Robert Johnson" Robert Johnson had died three days after the poisoning apparently "crawling on his hands an knees and barking like a dog". The fact that Johnson's actual death occurred three days later on August 16, 1938 was confirmed later when the death certificate was found.

However, the following conversation with Simon Napier, published in Blues Unlimited November 1963 adds more confusion to the story:

'Fessor Mojo's "Don't Start Me To Talkin"

"The first Question I put to Rice Miller was 'Do you remember Robert Johnson?'"

SBW — Yeah I remember him. I used to play with him, we toured around together.

SAN — He was with you when he died?

SBW — Yes, that's right. I'll tell you about it. Y'see he'd been recording down to Dallas, for Vocalion. He was never too good and we were coming home to Jackson, on the way to Memphis he died.

SAN — We heard he died in a car.

SBW — No, it was an ambulance, between Memphis and Jackson.

SAN — He was very young?

SBW — Very young, about nineteen or twenty I'd say. No more. [He was 27 according to the death certificate.]

SAN — What did he die of? Do you know?

SBW — Sure. He drank too much. He drank all the time. That what killed him. You ask Big Joe [Williams]. (I did - he said exactly the same, with no exhortation.)

SAN — Who'd he play with in those days?

SBW — He played with everyone. Lots o' people.

SAN — Elmore James?

SBW — Elmore, yes. Big Boy Crudup, we played with Muddy Waters then too.

At this point Sonny Boy broke off, saying "I'll tell you all about it. You write this down now." John Broven

Acknowledgments

wrote it all down. In "Blues Unlimited" soon you'll be able to read all about his great singer, along with Kurt Mohr's fine discography. Later, I transcribed my notes to the above and read it to Sonny Boy. He affirmed each answer again with "that's right".

Robert Johnson's last session, indeed in Dallas, was on June 20th, 1937. Seemingly he died soon after. [August 16, 1938 is on the death certificate still five years away from being found when this was written.]

[Comments in parentheses are Napier's, comments in brackets are Donoghue's.]

> **Sonny Boy Mystery #6 - Robert Johnson and Rice Miller At The Crossroads**—When did Rice Miller and Robert Johnson first meet? Did they go to the crossroads together? Separately? Was there ever a meeting at the crossroads? Can you tell me how you can sell your soul to the devil? What deals with the devil did Rice Miller and Robert Johnson make? Were they the same deals? I interviewed Honeyboy Edwards who was there. What can you tell me he hasn't already told me? Who killed Robert Johnson? Who was Robert Johnson's woman? Did Rice Miller have any complicity in Robert Johnson's death? Is there any evidence? Where did Robert Johnson actually die, Baptist Town as Honeyboy speculates (he was not there when Robert died) or on a plantation as is indicated on the reverse side of the death certificate)?

> **Sonny Boy Mystery #7 — <u>When did Sonny Boy Williamson start using the name "Sonny Boy Williamson"</u>?** Snooky Pryor claims that, in 1937, Sonny Boy Williamson II was using the name at a gig in Horseshoe AR. and that he told him "Don't Spill The Beans" about it. Can you confirm that he was using the name Sonny Boy Williamson before 1937?

KING BISCUIT TIME: THE GOOD AND BAD NEWS

In 1938, Robert Jr. Lockwood, long-time resident of nearby Marvell AR and stepson of the legendary Robert Johnson, first encountered a young Sonny Payne, at the gas station where Sonny's father worked. He inquired about a rumor that there would be a radio station started in Helena AR. That radio station, managed by a young educator Sam Anderson, finally went on the air in November of 1941.

Soon after, Sonny Payne secured a job with the station as a helper sweeping out the station, cleaning the records, etc.. Robert Jr. Lockwood and Sonny Boy Williamson came around asking about getting a show on the new station. They were referred to Max Moore of Interstate Grocery Company who had told station owner Sam Anderson he was interested in advertising his King Biscuit Flour to the local black audience. Lockwood and Williamson met with Moore who agreed to pay $12.50 a week for Sonny Boy Williamson to do the show, allegedly with a three-month trial period.

Soon after, Lockwood was added to the band followed by Peck Curtis and Dudlow Taylor on drums and piano, respectively. Later, Joe Willie Wilkens would be added on guitar when Robert Jr. Lockwood got his own, Mother's Best Flour - sponsored show.

Sonny Boy would remain on the show regularly from 1942 to 1944 or 1948. He would periodically return to the show over the years up until his death on May 25, 1965.

But having this highly popular show was a two edged sword for Sonny Boy. His show was successful but he was locked into using the "Sonny Boy Williamson" name simply because that was the role he chose to play. But he was now a highly-visible man who could be counted on to be at the KFFA studio in Helena AR at a specific time and, if he was found out to be an escaped convict, Rice Miller was too easy to find.

Even worse, after he began his "King Biscuit Time" broadcasts in late 1941, he became a man of great economic value to a white man; Max Moore of Interstate Grocery, whose King Biscuit Flour and Sonny Boy Corn meal he promoted. The law could have had him both ways! His drinking gave them more than enough good excuses to pick him up and hold him in jail until Max Moore or [later, from 1951-55] Lillian McMurry of Trumpet Records in Jackson MS, sent money to bail him out. It was a cruel game and I suspect that it became a cottage industry among some small town lawmen.

He was hounded by the "law" (who *could* have discovered his dark secret from his past) and they seemed to love to incarcerate him on a Saturday night knowing that the local grocery magnate would invariably bail him out so he could advertise his highly-profitable brand of flour and corn meal each week day. If that failed, there was always a plea to Lillian McMurry.

He was very much in love with Mattie, his wife, and yet he was a decided womanizer. He loved her dearly but could not seem to tell her so. He even tried to do so in song. In the end, this was the heartbreak of his life. When he came home to die, he never got tell her of his love.

He was an alcoholic. He needed three or four bottles of 100 proof Old Grand Dad to get him through a day. Toward the end, in 1963-65 or so, he could not keep food down if he did not have a drink first. Medically he was a serious disaster waiting to happen. By the time he left England at the end of April 1965, he knew he was a doomed man. He even confided that to Sonny Payne and other friends upon his return to Helena. By the morning of May 25, 1965, Sonny Boy had proven himself prophetic.

The indisputable proof of his drawing power, however, is found in the baking section of the local Delta supermarket. In spite of a decided preference for selling its own house brand of flour (a basic commodity in the Delta with its biscuit-driven cuisine), there is still a hefty shelf allocation for King Biscuit Flour and Sonny Boy Corn Meal, the sponsors of his still-running-over-fifty-years-later "King Biscuit Time", on Helena Arkansas' KFFA radio's noon-day soirée.

Ironically, in 1953, when a huge celebration of the 3,115th broadcast of the daily King Biscuit Time was planned, Sonny Boy was hired to entertain *but was not invited* to attend the celebration dinner at the Country Club. Blacks were certainly not invited to the Country Club.

You can feel his rage at this kind of treatment. Indeed, it became an underlying theme of Sonny Boy's sometimes unsubtle lyrics. He "ain't fattenin' frogs for snakes", warns you to "get your hand out of my pocket, there ain't nothing there that belongs to you", and cautions "let your conscience be your guide".

KING BISCUIT TIME MAKES BLUES HISTORY

The Peabody Award-winning "King Biscuit Time" started in 1941 or 1942 as a 15 minute noontime (12:45) radio show featuring the blues singer and harpist (harmonica player). First, it was just Sonny Boy Williamson performing solo and then, later, he added a guitarist or two, a pianist and drummer, The King Biscuit Entertainers or, in the language of the Delta, "The King Biscuit Boys."

It was among the first (Sonny Boy's WEBQ show in Eldorado IL in 1937 certainly preceded KFFA) radio shows ever to feature a black blues musician. There were earlier gospel shows including one featuring Clarksdale MS's Delta Rhythm Boys which aired on Sunday Mornings.

Actually Sonny Boy Williamson only appeared regularly on the show from 1942 to 1944 (or 1948) before the wanderlust and possibly the continuing troubles with the law or allegedly complaints from John Lee Williamson or Bluebird Records label drew him back on the road. Was it his need to continue to hide from the law or just wanderlust? We may never know.

He certainly was not in need of work. The jukes were rewarding him handsomely and he was earning as much as $75 a night. The radio show, while it only paid

$12.50 to $15.00 a week, allowed him ample opportunity to promote his appearances, making him a valuable and strong draw. The jukes were more than willing to respond with tempting advances for this man who had the attention of their world on this highly-visible radio show. No, for some reason, he wanted to become less visible; not invisible, but not such an obvious target for the law.

Maybe his celebrity just invited the "law" to harass this brilliant musician who was getting too "uppity", making too much money, and living too "high on the hog". His being a criminal was a tolerable situation, but being as low on the totem pole as a bluesman, being financially successful and willing to look the establishment directly in the eye at the risk of his own life was intolerable.

For Sonny Boy, the risk of being labeled a "crazy nigger" (excuse the decidedly politically incorrect language) presented the risk of being given a death sentence from which only the law could protect him. Realistically, the risk was minimal since he had a great economic value to his sponsor and, like a hard worker, he could do what he wanted against his own with impunity and the law's temptation to blackmail his benefactor by jailing him and constantly making appeals for "bail" was too profitable to risk "losing". Being "a man with dignity without an acceptable excuse" (being a teacher, a preacher or a ball player was an acceptable excuse, being a bluesman was not) was not an easy row to hoe in Clarksdale in the 1930s, '40s, 50's and 60's. His was a life of full of unspoken threats and intolerable stress.

Sonny Boy lived every day as if it were his last. I am sure he woke up most of his days penniless. He gambled compulsively and unwisely, he drank his whiskey continually, and as he was a very seductive performer even late in his life, he womanized with style. Wine, women and song is a powerful and expensive lifestyle. Add gambling to the mix and it can be an unsustainable lifestyle.

Sonny Boy, however, always knew that he could hustle a meal and a drink off of any cafe or juke owner who wanted him to play and draw a crowd. Each morning he could quickly—often in 10-15 minutes—raise his stake for the day. Give him his amplifier, his harp and a few minutes and he could make $25 to $50 within the hour.

But a recording career eluded him somehow. He sat back quietly while his friend and accompanist Robert Jr. Lockwood recorded in Chicago a decade before Sonny Boy would first record. He sat back as Lockwood moved his guitar to the more prestigious national network Mother's Best Flour show while he remained on the local King Biscuit show on the same station. He would return to Helena Arkansas and King Biscuit Time from time to time in the coming years, but the economic impact he made in those two plus years would keep the show running and the flour selling right up to today.

When you think about it rock 'n' roll and the blues tend to thrive for decades after very short periods of innovation; the dazzling two years between Robert Johnson's first records and his death, Elvis' 16 months with Sun Records, the short [1956-59] burst of rock energy which ended by 1959 with rock pioneers Elvis in the Army, Little Richard in the ministry, Chuck Berry in jail, Carl Perkins in the hospitals, Buddy Holly and Ritchie Valens in their graves and the irascible Jerry Lee Lewis in trouble for marrying his 13 year old cousin.

Sonny Boy's ability to build a radio show with a franchise strong enough to remain in business (and a thriving one at that) 65 years later based on a full-time tenure of probably less than three years is phenomenal. Sonny Boy and King Biscuit Time must have hit that Delta market like a tornado to remain strong 55 years later. King Biscuit Flour and Sonny Boy Corn Meal must have made millions for Interstate Grocery Company.

Sonny Boy had the urge to travel. He left his band to James Cotton in 1948 and left town to move to West Memphis to make a home with Mattie. He worked a radio show out of Belzoni MS and later out of West Memphis on KWEM. It was in West Memphis that his home burnt down as is celebrated in "West Memphis Blues" and it was where he first met Junior Wells.

Junior Wells described his first encounter with Sonny Boy Williamson, "I met him... I had been livin" in Chicago and I went back down to West Memphis, Arkansas on vacation, and Junior Parker, he was still livin" in Arkansas, so I knew Junior played harmonica also. And I asked Sonny Boy about showing me something on the harmonica, 'cause I'd saw him, he'd get on the cotton truck every morning to go chop cotton, but he wasn't choppin' cotton, he was just out there in the field with a hoe in his hand and he's gettin' paid for that, plus the man was payin' him, and he acted like he chopped a little cotton every now and then, and then he'd start blowing harmonica and singin' in the field. And this is what he was gettin' paid for.

"So one day I tried to talk him and he asked me he says, 'you wanna buy me a drink?' I said, 'yeah'. So he said 'Well, go get it.' And I went and got a half a pint and brought it back to him and, you know, he said, 'Are you lookin' at me?' I said, 'Yeah, I'm lookin' at ya.' He say, 'What I look like to you, a midget or something?' And I said, 'No'. He said, 'Well, you better go back and get a bigger bottle, 'cause that one won't do.' So I had to go back and get him a fifth. And I brought that back to him, you know.

"He started drinkin' that and he started showing me how to play the harmonica. He showed me about three times and that's all he would do. So I told him, I said, 'wait.' He said, 'Well, hey, let me tell you one thing', he said, 'in the first place you're stupid. And you're not gonna learn anything in the first place.' He said, 'I'm not gonna sit there and waste my time witcha, 'cause you're never gonna do nothin, 'cause you're stupid. And 'he says, 'you see that bottle of whiskey there?' I say, 'Yeah, I see it.' He say, 'And you bought that for me, didn't you?' I said, 'Yes, I did.' He said, 'Now, you know what you do?' He took his knife, he always took out his knife and licked it. He said, 'Now, if you taste that bottle, I'll cut your damn little throat.' He said, 'now get out of my face.'

"And I never had anything to hurt me that bad before in my life, as he hurt me then. So I hadn't saw him in 20-some odd years and I was playin' at Theresa's, and like I was doin, like a, Blue Monday matinee, me and Buddy Guy and a lot of other musicians and everybody come down and Theresa be to cook for ya, so everybody's eatin' and everybody's havin' a good time, and you know. And I came in and he was sittin' at the bar, so I went back in the, I come through the back side and went on up behind the bar to put my coat and things in Theresa's office.

'Fessor Mojo's "Don't Start Me To Talkin"

And he said, 'Hey, Junior.' I looked at him and kept on walkin'. So Theresa says, 'Junior, I know you're not gonna act that like to Sonny Boy'. I said, 'Tee, I don't have anything to say to him.' I said, 'You know what I told ya he did to me.' She said, 'Well, that don't make no difference here. He just come to see ya. You're the first thing he asked about when he come in.' I said, 'I don't care what he asked about.'

"So he asked me, he say, 'Junior, could I ask you one question.' I said, 'What's that?' He said, 'Now, you know, I know you're still mad at me about what I said to you and how I did you.' He said, But he said, 'I'm listening to what you played now.' He said, 'But you know why you playin' that way now?' I said, 'No, I don't, 'cause I'm playin' that way really because I know what I feel in my own soul and body.' He said, 'Well, now, do you know why I did you like I did you?' I said, 'No, I don't.' He said, 'Because you wouldn't be playin' as good as you are today if it don't be for me.' I said, 'You gotta be outta your mind. No I'm not.' He said, 'But you was pissed off with me so you were determined to show me that you could do this particular thing.' And I said... And he was right—I was determined to show him that I was gonna learn it right, and when he said that he said, 'Now, am I right or am I wrong?' I said, 'You right.' He said, 'Now can we have a drink together? I'm buying this time!' After that, we was okay with each other."

I then asked Junior if that meant they were close friends. Did Sonny Boy open up to you? Did he ever explain why he needed to carry that knife. "No, he didn't. He never did. And I never did ask him! You know, 'cause I figured, you know, if he's sittin' there drinkin' a fifth of whiskey, and I mean he could drink a whole fifth of whiskey and you didn't see him stagger around or nothing. So I figured that I didn't want to get close to it no way, he be drinkin' that much alcohol. I figured he might go off. So, I didn't."

Even his close friends learned to keep their distance from Sonny Boy.

SONNY BOY IS DISCOVERED BY LILLIAN MCMURRY

Considering Sonny Boy's economic impact on the Helena AR market in the early forties it is nothing short of incredible to discover that Sonny Boy was not recorded until 1951. By then he was possibly past his prime and in his forties or fifties.

In fact, it was a bit of a fluke that he was discovered at all. Lillian McMurry of Trumpet Records heard about him from Curtis Dossett, a friend of the family who owned theaters around Mississippi. He had heard of Sonny Boy playing between shows and acts in a little theater in the Delta. He didn't even know his name.

So, one Sunday afternoon, he, Mrs. McMurry and her brother drove north into the Delta to find this man so she could record him. At the intersection of Routes 49 East and West, she found Ernie Fields and his orchestra playing a show. When asked, Ernie said "I know him and he's great." The searched all day and finally found his wife Mattie in Belzoni. She recognized who Mrs. McMurry was from the Record Mart store's ads on WRBC where she advertised and promised to send her husband, Sonny Boy Williamson to Jackson to record.

'Fessor Mojo's "Don't Start Me To Talkin"

Mrs. McMurry had never heard him play and, in fact, never did see him perform outside of the studio but she was convinced she wanted to record him. When he showed up to record with his band, he was well-dressed "Sonny Boy always went neat!" she would later say. A very special musical relationship began, one that would put both in the blues history books.

Sonny Boy would continue record for Trumpet Records until 1954 both under his own name and on some of Trumpet's other biggest hits, including "Eyesight To The Blind" [which is currently playing on Broadway in New York in "Tommy" as I write this book], the blockbuster two-sided hit "Mighty Long Time" backed with "Nine Below Zero", " West Memphis Blues", "Pontiac Blues", (the 30th Robert Johnson song alluded to in the movie "Crossroads") "Mr. Downchild", "She Brought Life Back To The Dead", "Keep It To Yourself", and three of Lillian McMurry's songs "Red Hot Kisses", "From The Bottom" and "No Nights By Myself" plus Trumpet's biggest-seller (and the only song Elmore had prepared to her satisfaction on the day after he signed an exclusive contract with Trumpet, ironically his last for Trumpet), Elmore James' "Dust My Broom" backed with Bobo "Slim" Thomas's "Catfish Blues" and Big Boy Crudup's "Gonna Find My Baby".

In 1955, Trumpet went out of business. Lillian McMurry sold Sonny Boy Williamson's contract to Buster Williams, owner of Plastic Products, their pressing plant, in cancellation of a huge back debt to the firm. Williams then sold the contract to Chess Records and Sonny Boy became a Chess artist.

NEXT STOP CHICAGO!

The first Chess recording session on August 12, 1955 was a sign of things to come. Muddy Waters himself and his whole band backed up Sonny Boy and propelled him to #3 on the R&B charts with "Don't Start Me To Talkin'". He would see chart action again in 1956 with "Keep It To Yourself" and finally in 1963 with [basically the "Green Onions" riff] "Help Me". For much of the time he was on Chess, his records competed with and often outsold even Muddy Waters.

Sonny Boy seldom had a real band of his own, except possibly for Sam Carr and Frank Frost, who backed him up from 1956-59 in the Delta and later when he returned from Europe. His later sessions would be with the Chess rhythm section featuring his old King Biscuit Time comrade Robert Jr. Lockwood and Luther Tucker on guitar, Otis Spann on piano, Willie Dixon on bass and Fred Below on drums. On later sessions Lafayette Leake sat in on piano, Matt Murphy or Eugene Pierson on guitar and Odie Payne on drums. Toward the end of his tenure, he used Buddy Guy's band, with Billy Emerson's organ added on "Help Me" and "Bring It On Home".

Junior Wells described how Sonny Boy would set up for a gig: "He didn't bother nobody. He didn't bother nobody at all. He just do what I said, he would just do what I say he do. He'd lay his towel out, put his cigarettes down, take a fifth of whiskey and put it up there, had the people bring him his ice, take his knife, lick it, and put it down there. He said, 'Now if anybody want a drink, I'll buy ya one, but don't touch nothin up here.'"

Given that Sonny Boy had seen Robert Johnson die from drinking poisoned whiskey, Sonny Boy always drank from a sealed bottle and never shared that bottle with anyone.

During his time on Chess he lived variously in Detroit (twice), Cleveland and Milwaukee.

The bulk of his major recordings are on Chess. It encompasses a body of work including 89 Chess recordings and alternative takes (not including the eleven takes on the legendary "Little Village" alone).

CHICAGO MAY NOT HAVE BEEN SONNY'S "KIND OF TOWN"

Chicago had its drawbacks for Sonny Boy II, however, because it was the home base of John Lee "Sonny Boy" Williamson I during his recording years up until his death in 1948. [For the record, he apparently was not stabbed with an icepick but he was hit on the head with a piece of concrete, staggered to his home, collapsed in the arms of his wife and died in his sleep without treatment.]

Sonny Boy II (Rice Miller) did not start to record until 1951 or three years after Sonny Boy I's death. But, he did have the temerity to record as "Sonny Boy Williams" on a Tampa Red recording session on Bluebird, Sonny Boy I's label. But Sonny Boy I was very popular in Chicago and some fans resented Sonny Boy II's use of his name. This is probably why posters exist listing "Sonny Boy Williams" as appearing with Elmore James for example. They saw right through that one. I asked Sonny Boy I fan and blues harpist Billy Boy Arnold "What kind of reception did Rice Miller get when he would play the Chicago clubs?" It was not always a welcome one.

"Well I'll tell you one time in particular. He had came here to record for Chess, and he was playin' at Ricky's Show Lounge, and I came down there that night, and when I got there, Rice Miller's white shirt was bloody, soaked with blood. He was sitting on the band stand. He has Luther [Tucker with whom] he had just recorded. He had Luther Tucker on guitar, whoever was playin' with Little Walter and Walter was off that night and they had recorded with Rice Miller, and they was playin' with him at Ricky's Show Lounge," Billy Boy Arnold told me.

"Some guy grabbed him by the shirt, by the, I mean by the tie, slung him off the band stand and he hit his nose on the post. His shirt was all bloody. By the time Rice Miller got his knife out of his pocket, the guy had ran out the club! We walked in right just as it happened. Rice Miller was all bloody. He say, I gotta go to the house and get another shirt. Now, what somebody told me was, see, John Lee Williamson lived in Chicago and was, had a lot of friends and people remembered him. And a lot of people resented him [Rice Miller] calling hisself 'Sonny Boy Williamson'."

Sonny Boy couldn't even get a break by "dressing neat". Billy Boy Arnold also reports that in 1965 a hostile M. C. and apparently some of the audience (including Billy Boy) at the Regal Theater misread his sartorial style and took a potshot at Sonny Boy's expensive custom-made English suit , "And the emcee said, 'Hey, Sonny Boy, you gotta get you a Chicago suit!' He had on one them back numbers from 1941, you know. So he was behind time. He didn't, he didn't know how to dress... I mean, nobody woulda showed up in a 1941 suit in 1965 at the Regal Theater!"

Chicago did not always put out a welcome mat for Sonny Boy.

SONNY BOY INFLUENCES THE BEATLES

Recently, I was watching The Beatles Anthology (the ten-hour documentary, not the shorter one that ran on American TV) and I watched The Beatles perform their first hit, "Love Me Do". What struck me as familiar was the way John Lennon held his harmonica—it was very similar to the way Sonny Boy held his! The left hand makes a sandwich of the harmonica and the right hand places its fingertips in the front of the harp.

Is it possible that Sonny Boy Williamson II had taught John Lennon to play the harp? I had heard that The Beatles were given front row seats for the American Folk Blues Festival shows. However, "Love Me Do" was recorded in 1962—actually three times each with a different drummer (session drummer Alan White, Peter Best and Ringo Starr) and the first was recorded on June 6, 1962, fifteen months before Sonny Boy arrived on the shores of England and probably long before he even knew he was coming.

Then it hit me. Delbert McClinton was rumored to have taught John Lennon how to play harmonica. Delbert was the harp player on Bruce Channel's "Hey Baby!" hit in 1962.

In a recent issue of Goldmine, McClinton tells the story about one night on his trip to England with Bruce Channel in early 1962 ;"So this particular night, to tell God's truth, I couldn't say that it was John, but I know it was one of the Beatles because I had been listening to them. History says it was John. The only reason I know it was one of the Beatles was that they had on these fine, black leather suites, and I flipped out on them. I asked where they got them, and the next day, I went to London and bought a jacket like theirs. History's been saying all this time I taught John Lennon how to play the harmonica. I only know it was one of the Beatles. But, to sit here and bare-faced tell the truth, I ain't got no clue who it was."

That answers the question of who taught Lennon to play harp, but who taught Delbert to play? Who were his influences on harp?

"For the next two years [1961-63] I was fortunate enough to work with Jimmy Reed a lot, and with Buster Brown, Sonny Boy (Williamson), Howlin' Wolf, Joe Turner, Joe Tex, Bo Diddley. Backing them up in this club. We'd even do Friday and Saturday night in Fort Worth, and on Sunday we'd drive to Oklahoma, up around Lawton, and play Sunday night in black clubs with Sonny Boy....It was wonderful and what makes it so good was I knew it at the time. I knew I was in the middle of something that you don't fall into everyday. So I got as much time with these guys as I could—maybe not talking to the—but sitting in their presence. And they'd show me things."

Is it possible that Sonny Boy taught Delbert to hold the harp the way Lennon does? Stay tuned because Delbert's answer will probably be in our video documentary. I just thought you'd enjoy the speculation. If it's true, Europe was more than ready for Sonny Boy to arrive and arrive he did in the early fall of 1963. I am getting ahead of my story.

EUROPE BECKONS

Willie Dixon and Memphis Slim had, by the mid-1950s, gotten the idea that there was good work for bluesmen in Europe. In 1958 and 1959 Muddy Waters and Otis Spann had been invited to play England. The 1958 tour featuring Muddy's electric guitar, now standard equipment for his Chicago gigs, was greeted by reviews of "screaming guitars and howling pianos". The British, used to the acoustic blues sound of Big Bill Broonzy, did not expect bluesmen to play electric guitars. Sensitive to the British market, in 1959, Muddy left his electric guitar in Chicago only to be asked where it was as the rockers got used to the new sound. The same impact would happen years later on the folk festival circuit in America when the Butterfield Blues Band's electric sound inspired by Muddy Waters' band took the center stage.

By 1962, the American Negro Blues Festival had been started. The following year, the 1963 American Folk Blues Festival booked by Willie Dixon invited Sonny Boy Williamson to join Muddy Waters, Victoria Spivey, Memphis Slim, Big Joe Williams, Lonnie Johnson, Otis Spann, Billie Stepney and Willie Dixon in the September European tour. Sonny Boy was a huge hit and found himself playing the concert halls of Europe.

Giorgio Gomelsky tells us (in the liner notes to his BYG records release) about a special evening during Sonny Boy's first visit to England. "From all accounts, though, Sonny Boy was *indefatigable* on his European jaunt—especially during a sold-out British tour.

"In Croydon, there was a small pub where the Yardbirds played—at the time, completely unknown," remembers Lippman, "Sonny Boy and myself, after the concert we usually went somewhere to hear music, because Sonny Boy liked to jam with his harmonica. So we went to this club and Sonny Boy sat in, and he was so enthusiastic about the very young Eric Clapton, who was then 17 years old. I decided when the tour's over, Sonny Boy would return to England and I would record him with the Yardbirds"

"Sonny Boy was fantastic." says Lippman "First of all, I got shocked at how much he drank. But after a while, I understood that he needed his bottle of whiskey, and then he performed perfectly. He was a great success.

"I only had a problem one time. He was drinking *more* than one bottle. He was drinking two or three bottles. You know what happened then? He didn't want to leave the stage! He played for hours."

Sonny Boy had discovered the Yardbirds and more importantly Eric Clapton. Later he would record with the Yardbirds, the Animals and a group including Brian Auger and the Trinity and a young Jimmy Page.

After arriving in Europe in September, he was recording prolifically with many of his tour mates; Victoria Spivey and Memphis Slim. He even made a short film for Swedish TV and appeared on the AFBF's "I Hear the Blues" special for Grenada TV. By January he was being featured with British Trad star Chris Barber. In February of 1964 he was in Birmingham with the Yardbirds. By the end of April he was back in Chicago for a Chess session, Chess having reawakened to his record potential after the success in Europe. Frankly, they were probably jealous that he had gotten so much attention from competitors.

A month later, in May 1964, he was back in Europe playing The Free Trade Hall in Manchester England with The Chris Barber Band. By August he was back in the studio for his final Chess records session in Chicago.

In September 1964, he returned for the 1964 American Folk Blues Festival Tour, this time with Sunnyland Slim, Howlin' Wolf, Hubert Sumlin, John Fred Barbee, Lightnin' Hopkins, Sleepy John Estes and Hammie Nixon, Clifton James, Sugar Pie DeSanto and Mae Mercer and the ubiquitous Willie Dixon. Touring with Sleepy John Estes was Delmark Records' Bob Koester and with Lightnin' Hopkins was Arhoolie Records' Chris Strachwitz.

Strachwitz described traveling with Sonny Boy on the American Folk Blues Festival tour in 1964. "I had the pleasure of first meeting Sonny Boy really when we went to Europe on that trip in '64, I guess it was, when I went there with Lightnin' because he wouldn't travel unless I went with him. And on the trip was Sonny Boy Williamson, and Howlin' Wolf, and I think Buddy...,no, no it wasn't Buddy, I forgot who the guitar player was [Hubert Sumlin]. Anyway, that was, that was how I got to know him.

"And then we would travel on buses, you know... actually, the very first day I think when we arrived in Munich, I'll never forget that one. They would meet us with either a limousine or some kind of a vehicle that would pick us up, you know. And this was always a fairly large bus, one of those tourist buses, and there was a microphone right in the front, you know, right next to the driver.

"And Sonny Boy just spotted that right away and grabbed that microphone, and from the airport all the way to the hotel, which was at least a half-hour ride, he just, by himself, I don't even know whether he even blew the harmonica, but just this verbal... Filthiest version of the Dirty Dozens I have ever encountered in my life! And I remember there was one woman on the tour, Sugar Pie DeSanto, and I mean she was just curling over, and to them guys it was just... I sure wish I would have had a song snatcher [video camera] in those days with me like we have now, you know. But it just went out in the air.

"But I've never heard anything like it. He made just like he would on his radio programs, you know. But he knew he was just talking to us and it was just unreal!

"And then he would usually room with Sunnyland Slim on this trip. I remember in Sweden one night I told him I'd like to go eat dinner with him, you know, and knocked on their door, and I think Sunnyland opened up and the whole room was just filled with steam. 'What you guys all doin'?' 'Ah, man, we, we're cooking that chicken right here in a coffee pot, you see. Man, we're gonna have that chicken right here. Do you wanna have some of it?' I said, 'well, you know, I believe I better go eat downstairs.' And I should've eaten with them. And, you know, just different occasions like that.

"And one time in Sweden I think he had an interview scheduled with this Swedish, one of the biggest dailies, and we were all sittin around, you know, like here eating breakfast and Sonny Boy comes down and we all said, 'where you goin' Sonny Boy?' 'Oh, I'm goin' to a blues paper and tell bullcorn.' And he had that gruff voice, almost like Wolf, you know."

Ironically it was all that "bull corn" that Sonny Boy told that turned later researchers off to Sonny Boy. He just told too many lies. From that time right up to today, there has been precious little active research into Sonny Boy Williamson II's life, at least in print.

For example, we have finally debunked (maybe?) one of Sonny Boy's claims; to have played on the Grand Ole Opry back in the thirties. In fact, he claimed that he has participated in a jam fellow harp players Lonnie Glosson (a white country musician) and Deford Bailey (the black harp player who was featured on the Grand Ole Opry from 1929 to 1941) on the stage of the Grand Ole Opry in Nashville! (A recording of that historic session, which may exist, would pre-date his first recordings by a decade and a half! See Sonny Boy Mystery #8.).

As it turned out, we found Lonnie Glosson who told us he did jam with Sonny Boy once—at a fair in Memphis. Charles Wolfe, Deford Bailey's biographer knew nothing of such an encounter with Deford Bailey but suggested that it could have happened on "Night Train", a local Nashville TV show of the '50s and '60s sponsored by Randy's Records on WLAC-TV. (So far, nothing has turned up to confirm that hunch.)

> **Sonny Boy Mystery #8 — Did Sonny Boy really jam with Glosson and Bailey?** If you know when and where he did (unless it was that fair in Memphis) let us know.

"Yeah." Strachwitz continued "He had a kind of a gruff voice like, like Wolf did, you know, naturally. And we asked him where he was going, and he says he's got a interview to do, you know, with the newspaper or somethin. And, well, we said, 'well, we'll see you when you get back.' Well, we were still sittin there when he got back about two hours later, and I was just curious, I asked him, what did you tell 'em, you know? Because we all knew him, that he would never tell the same story twice. And I don't think anybody knew anything about him. And he said, 'Well, you know, I gave 'em some of the bullshit and told 'em how long my dick was and all that stuff they wanted to know!'"

I asked Chris why Sonny Boy was always telling different stories.

"No. But, I mean, we, we had the clue that, you know, he figured his past is past and its nothing look back to. I heard, they all said he had spent some time in prison, you know, and stuff, and, I mean, he seemed like a natural born entertainer or somebody who developed an act, you know, that took him through this world. And he knew just what to do, where, and when, and I think he enjoyed the fact that he could make up stories faster than they could think of their questions, you know.

"And he was, in that way he was just like Bukka White. You know, if you ever met him, he would make up tales at the drop of a hat. They just came out of the sky, as he called them. And I think Sonny Boy was something like that. And I know he was because, you know, his records were so straight, actually. They were usually fairly well-developed pieces, that I thought he would do fairly much the same way. But it was an eye opener when, when I heard him in Europe then where he would be improvising stuff, just like Lightnin' did, and so on. And I was really amazed that somebody like Willie Dixon organized band pieces like he recorded.

"Because to me, that, that was the thing on that microphone going in, in to Munich. I mean, it was just totally ad-libbing this fantasy of his, you know. And it just... I'm sure he had maybe practiced it once before, but a lot of it, I think, just came spontaneously. And always there was... As I say, I wish I'd have caught it, but... In his performances almost every night there was some reference about what happened that day or, or why these pretty girls here would, how the whiskey store was hard to find, or something would be coming in. I don't really remember, you know, exactly how. But he was just what can I say. He was an incredible improviser, you know. His whole energy was focused on, on what to put out of his mouth, what to sing or tell you."

I asked if he was close to the other musicians. Did he seem to open up to them? "He would be... Not that I know, because I didn't really spend much time with him and Sunnyland together, you know. They would be, I don't know what they were talking about, really. All I can think of probably just old bullcorn stories, you know.

"But his mind was going all the time, you know, and people treated him pretty royally, so he, he figured he gotta do something there and they give him this biggest damn whiskey bottle I've ever seen, it was about this big, in Berlin, I guess. And he had it on the bus.

"And but he was an improviser, and you can hear it on those records he made for Knudson in Denmark, you know, in Storyville, where he just has Matt Murphy with Memphis Slim on piano. And he talks about going up and down the Rhine and just making up stuff, you know."

In October 1964 he would record on sessions in Hamburg and Munich appear on a TV Show in Baden-Baden called American Folk Blues Festival 1964 with all of the cast except Sugar Pie DeSanto. The show would open with him playing "Bye Bye Bird" on a set which could be mistaken for downtown Helena AR, playing "In My Younger Days" with Sunnyland Slim, Clifton James, Willie Dixon and Hubert Sumlin, playing beside a more than slightly stoned Mae Mercer and off camera on one of Howlin' Wolf's blues.

He would stay in Europe until late April 1965 when Giorgio Gomelsky arranged a final studio session with Jimmy Page (Clapton was apparently not to be found at the time), Brian Auger and the Trinity (an organ trio) and two jazz saxes, Joe Harriott and Alan Skidmore. It has the sound of a hastily arranged experimental session, more pop that blues. Sonny Boy was ready to join even the mod rockers for a romp. His final session includes "Don't Send Me No Flowers"

He returned to the U. S. and Helena AR that day. On arrival he informed his longtime friend, "Sunshine" Sonny Payne that we had returned home to die. Sonny tried to argue with him on the issue but Sonny Boy knew he was on his last legs.

Chris Strachwitz picks up the story in Helena AR in May of 1965.

"And then later on when I met him again in Helena, Arkansas, there on that radio program, you know, [The only King Biscuit Time program with Sonny Boy Williamson ever recorded was made with Strachwitz' mike tied to the big old mike in which the musicians played. You could hear the announcer in the background as it is a studio mike. That show is on the Arhoolie King Biscuit Time CD only.] he would be announcing and telling people where he's gonna be that night. And there, people didn't really believe that he had played for concerts like that, like when you hear that little record, you know, the announcer says he just came back from Europe playing for the Armed Forces. He didn't play for no Armed Forces! This was for big concert halls all over Europe, you know, because blues were becoming a really popular music over there. And, ah, so they were really stars."

But there was still one more musical adventure ahead of him.

Strachwitz continues his story. "Oh, actually, I remember, you know, when we were in Helena... That's right, there was a rock band from Canada that was down there also taking the pilgrimage to visit him. They had absolutely admired him. I don't remember the name of the band, but they were from Canada. And they said, Oh, yeah, we just admire Sonny Boy. And I told them where, where he, he was staying. I remember I ran into them the next day as I was leaving, and I forgot if they wanted to record with him or not."

For those of you who have seen The Band's 1978 "The Last Waltz" movie and remember Robbie Robertson's story of their jam with Sonny Boy and his spitting blood in a can during the jam, you already know who the band was. It was Levon and the Hawks. Levon was Levon Helm and this was the group that would rename themselves The Band (from Big Pink). They jammed with Sonny Boy that night and made big plans to tour with him. Both artists left on a high.

> **Sonny Boy Mystery #9 - The Hawks' (The Band's) Jam With Sonny Boy in May of 1965.** Did they jam only on one night (which night?) or several nights? Did they play only at the Rainbow Inn Motel in West Helena as claimed in Levon's book or did they jam a lot of places over a few days? Who were Sonny Boy's people who wrote to The Hawks in Somers Point NJ.? How soon afterwards did Sonny Boy die? What did they play? Where did they play?

The next month they were playing at Tony Mart's in Somers Point NJ (my favorite summertime hangout for six years before the Hawks arrived). While there they got a letter from "Sonny Boy's people" telling them of Sonny Boy Williamson II's death on May 25, 1965. They also got a call from Bob Dylan asking them to join him at the Hollywood Bowl September 3, 1965. Robbie Robertson and Levon Helm would eventually join him August 28, 1965 at Forest Hills Tennis Stadium and the full band would find him in Columbia Studios in early October of 1965. By the following Spring The Hawks (minus Levon and with Mickey Jones on drums) would be setting the woods on fire in Europe. Electric folk music had arrived if you could hear it above the all the booing..

One can only imagine what Dylan would have sounded like if Sonny Boy had lived another year or two to be with The Hawks when they joined Dylan. Don't discount the possibility. The elderly blues/jazz fiddler Papa John Creach was later to join with the Jefferson Airplane and toured with spin-off band Hot Tuna for years until his death in the '90s.

It was not to be. On the morning of May 25, 1965 Sonny Boy did not show up at the studios for King Biscuit Time. The announcer sent James "Peck' Curtis to rouse him for the show. Curtis found Sonny Boy Williamson II, "Rice" Miller dead in his bed in his apartment 421 1/2 Elm Street in Helena AR. He has apparently died in his sleep about 4:00 AM that morning.

The irony is that some of his misrepresentation survived him and he took some more of his secrets with him. His death certificate cites Jim "Williamson" as his father, the name he claimed was his excuse for identifying himself as "The Only Sonny Boy, THE Sonny Boy. There ain't no other one but me" or "Mr. Original Sonny Boy Williamson" as he had told Archie Shepp. It would be fifteen years, until 1980, before Lillian McMurry would discover that the man she knew as Willie "Sonny Boy" Williamson was really Aleck "Rice" Miller, a fact known to all of his fellow musicians for decades. (She knew he wasn't the Sonny Boy Williamson who recorded "Good Morning Little School Girl" but she believed that his name was "Williamson.") Precisely when his widow Mattie learn that the man she married as Willie "Sonny Boy" Williamson had yet another name is a fact still to be ascertained.

> **Sonny Boy Mystery #10 - When did Mattie discover her husband's real name?** Was it before she married him, after his death or did she know all along? What is her explanation for his hiding behind another man's name?

I think that Morris Gist, proprietor of Gist's Music on Cherry Street in Helena AR sums up Sonny Boy's special sense of dignity even through the cloud of alcoholism and the cage of racism in which he lived.

I asked him "What do you think Sonny Boy was angry about?"

His answer touched me "Oh I've thought since, since the 60's, that Sonny Boy was probably one of the first activists. The black people who really resented the subjugation by the white community, the unfairness of it. And I think he, he was probably braver in one sense than those people who marched in Alabama. Because if he resisted in those days, he actually put his life and physical well-being in jeopardy. There was no way he could say no to any authority in the community, any of the white people, almost, and certainly none of the law enforcement people of the community. Because they had the power of, judge and jury and executioner in those days, on those black people. So, I think he was one of the first who, who actually exhibited his resentment of that situation."

In a world turned upside down by poverty, segregation, exploitation and illiteracy, Sonny Boy Williamson found the courage to stand tall and proud.

Sonny Boy Williamson II was a man of mystery. He was an escaped convict who became an international blues star using another man's name. And, if I am correct, that is only the beginning of the story of Sonny Boy Williamson II.

'Fessor Mojo's "Don't Start Me To Talkin"

9/7/96
DISCOGRAPHY
copyright William E. Donoghue 1996 (sonnyboy@donoghue.com)

SONNY BOY WILLIAMSON No. 2

(ALECK FORD AKA "RICE" MILLER)

[It is rumored that in the late 1940s, Sonny Boy Williamson and Elmore James recorded some commercials for Talaho Syrup which aired on a WGVM, Greenville MS and WAZF, Yazoo City MS from which they did a weekly radio show.]

[Sonny Boy also claimed to have made or been recorded on several Pre-War blues recordings on various labels. No record has been found of these recordings, nor are his claims supported in any way. He was, according the Honeyboy Edwards, taken over to Jackson MS to audition for H. C. Speir in late December of 1937 but no records were made. **"You take right in, in '37 after Robert come in to Greenwood, and me and Sonny Boy and Tommy McClennan takin off and went to Jackson, and we was supposed to record for H. C. Speir, old**

'Fessor Mojo's "Don't Start Me To Talkin"

man Speir in Jackson, Mississippi. Me and Sonny Boy, Tommy, and Big Walter Horton, we went and... Mr. Speir, he lives on West 9th Street there in Jackson, Mississippi. And we was supposed to record for Mr. Speir and we got there so, so close to Christmas, it, it was about five or six days to Christmas, and we didn't get a chance to record for the holidays, but he paid us the expenses and everything, everything. " Honeyboy Edwards.]

v/hca with Willie Love, p; Elmore James, g; Joe Willie Wilkens, g; Joe Dyson, d.
Jackson MS 4 Jan 1951

DRC 15	Eyesight to the blind	Tpt 129
DRC 16	Crazy about you baby	-
DRC 17	Stop Crying	Trumpet unissued
DRC 18	Do what you wanna	-
DRC 19	Cool, cool blues	-
DRC 20	Come on back blues	-
DRC 21	I cross my heart	-
DRC 22	West Memphis Bluew	-

(Note: the above masters were destroyed in a fire and subsequently re-recorded.)

v/hca with Willie Love, p; unk., g; Henry Reed, b; Joe Dyson, d.
Jackson MS 12 Mar 1951

DRC 15-2	Eyesight to the blind	Tpt. 129, BC LP 9, Arh LP 2020
DRC 16-2	Crazy about you baby	- , - , -

v/hca with Elmore James, g; Henry Reed, b; Joe Dyson, d.
Jackson MS, 10 Jul 1951

DRC 17	Stop Crying	Tpt unissued
DRC 18	Do it if you wanna	-
DRC 19	Cool, cool blues	-
DRC 20	Come on back home	-
DRC 21	West Memphis blues	-
DRC 45	Sonny Boy's Christmas blues	-
DRC 46	Pontiac Blues	-

BOBO "SLIM" THOMAS
(& SONNY BOY WILLIAMSON)

Bobo "Slim" Thomas [Andrew Thomas] Sonny Boy Williamson, hca; Leonard Ware, b.
Jackson MS 24 July 1951

DRC-52	Catfish Blues (I wish I were a catfish)	Tpt 146, Ace 508, Jewel 783, Nthk LP 109, ALCD 2803

SONNY BOY WILLIAMSON,
HIS HARMONICA & HOUSEROCKERS (140,144)

v/hca with Willie Love, p; Dave Campbell, p-1; Elmore James, g; Joe Willie Wilkens, g; Leonard Ware, b, unk., d.
Jackson MS, 5 Aug 1951

DRC 17	Stop Crying	Tpt 140, BC LP 9, Arh LP 2020
DRC 18	Do it if you wanna	Trp 139
DRC 19	Cool, cool blues-1	-
DRC 20	Come on back home	Trp 140

DRC 21	I cross my heart	Trp 144
DRC 22	West Memphis blues	-
DRC 45	Sonny Boy's Christmas blues	Trp 145
DRC 46	Pontiac Blues	-

(Note: DRC 17/22 also mastered as ACA 2031, 2024/3, 2032, 2030/29 resp: DRC 45/46 as ACA 2027, & 2025 resp.)

ELMORE JAMES
(WITH SONNY BOY WILLIAMSON)

v/g, Sonny Boy Williamson, hca; Leonard Ware, b.
Jackson MS 5 Aug 1951

DRC 53	Dust My Broom	Tpt, Arh CD 310

SONNY BOY WILLIAMSON,
HIS HARMONICA & HOUSEROCKERS
or
SONNY BOY WILLIAMSON
& HIS HOUSEROCKERS (215)

v/hca with Willie Love, p-1; Elmore James, g; Joe Willie Wilkens, g (except -2); Cliff Givens, vocal b; Joe Dyson, d - 3.
Jackson MS, 4 Dec 1951

DRC 88	Mighty long time-2	Tpt 166, BC LP 9, Arh 2020
DRC 89	Nine below zero -1,2,3	- , - , -
DRC 90	She brought life back to the dead-1	Tpt 215
45-DRC-90	She brought life back to the dead (alt tk)-1	Tpt 215, LP 801
DRC 91	Too close together -3	Tpt 212, BC LP 9, Arh 2020

DRC 92	Stop now baby -3	Tpt 168,	-	,	-
DRC 93	Mr. Down Child -3	-	,	-	,	-

(Note: DRC 90 & 45-90 were 78 & 45 rpm versions resp. DRC 88/90 are mastered on ACA 2119/7/8 resp: 45-DRC 90 as ACA 45-2118, DRC 91/3 as ACA 2122/0/1 resp.)

ROBERT "DUDLOW" TAYLOR
(W/ SONNY BOY WILLIAMSON)

v/p with Sonny Boy Williamson, hca; Elmon Mickle, b; Peck Curtis, d.
Helena AK 22 Jan 1952

Porkina blues	unissued
Lonesome	Kent LP 9007
I know	unissued
Old Helena blues	Kent LP 9007
Depot agent blues	unissued

JAMES "PECK" CURTIS
(W/SONNY BOY WILLIAMSON)

v/d with Sonny Boy Williamson, hca; Elmon Mickle, hca; Robert "Dudlow" Taylor, p; poss W. C. Clay, g.
Helena AK 22 Jan 1952

Jerusalem blues	Kent LP 9007
Bus fare	unisssued

ARTHUR "BIG BOY" CRUDUP & SONNY BOY WILLIAMSON

Arthur "Big Boy" Crudup, v/g; Sonny Boy Williamson, hca; Joe Willie Wilkens, g; "Sam" bass
Jackson MS, 28 Aug 1952

Make a little love with me	Trp , ALCD 2803
Gonna find my baby	Trp , ALCD 2803

---

v/hca with Bernard Williams, Willie Kyle, Carlton Wells, saxes, J. W. Walker, p; Joe Willie Wilkens, g; unk, b; Oneal Hudson, d. Omit two saxes -1)
Jackson MS, 23 Mar 1953

DRC 180	Car hop (inst.) -1	Tpt 212, LP 801, Blues Ball LP 2004, PV(J) PCD 2183
	She's crazy	unissued
	"309"	- PV(J) PCD 2183
	Sonny's rhythm	unissued
	City of New Orleans	-
	Clowning with the world	-

(Note: DRC 180 also mastered as ACA 2560)

---

v/hca with Richard Lillie, ts; Willie Love, p; Lester Williams, g; Rusty Alfred, b; Buck Hinson, d.
Houston TX, 14 Apr 1953

tk 1	She's crazy	Tpt LP 801, PV(J) PCD 2183
tk 2	She's crazy	Tpt LP 700, ALCD 2700

	"309"	-
tk 1	Sonny's rhythm	-
tk 2	Sonny's rhythm	Tpt LP 801
	City of New Orleans	Tpt LP 700, ALCD 2700
	Clowning with the world	unissued

Tampa Red

v/g with Sonny Boy Williamson, hca; Johnny Jones, v-1/p; Willie Lacey, g; Ranson Knowling, b; Odie Payne, d
Chicago IL 1 Sept 1953

E3-VB0268	We don't get along no more	unissued
E3-VB0269	So crazy about you baby - 1	Vic 20-5523, LP 2-5501
E3-VB0270-1	So much trouble	- , BC LP 25
E3-VB0271-1	If she don't come back	Vic 20-5594

"SONNY BOY" WILLIAMSON & HIS HOUSEROCKERS or HIS ORCHESTRA (Tpt 216)
or
"SONNY BOY" WILLIAMSON (Ace)

v/hca; David Campbell, p; James Williams, g; Bernard "Bunny" Williams, ts; Herman Fowlkes, b; Oneal Hudson, d; Frank Crawford, cuaraches-1
Jackson MS 24 October 1953

DRC 185	Gettin out of town-1	Tpt 215, LP 801
DRC 186-1	Keep it to yourself	PV(J) CD 2183, ALCD 2700
DRC 186-2	Keep it to yourself	Tpt LP 700
DRC 187	Red hot kisses	Tpt 216, :LP 801, Blues Ball LP 2004, PV(J) 2183

'Fessor Mojo's "Don't Start Me To Talkin"

DRC 188-4 Going in your direction   PV(J) CD 2183
DRC 188-5 Going in your direction   Tpt 216, :LP 801, Blues
                                      Ball LP 2004

(Note: DRC 183/8 also mastered as ACA 2772, 2770, 2771 & 2769 resp.)

———

v/hca with Dave Campbell, p; J. V. Turner, g; Johnny Morgan, b; Junior Blackman; d.
Jackson MS 2 Nov 1954

DRC 211   Empty bedroom   Tpt 228, LP 801, PV(J) 2183
DRC 214-1 Clowning with the world(inst) Tpt LP 700, PV(J) 2183
DRC 214-2 Clowning with the world
          (Boppin with Sonny) [inst] Ace 511, Tpt LP 801,
                                      ALCD 2700, PV(J) 2183
DRC 215   I'm not beggin' nobody   Tpt LP 700, ALCD 2700,
                                    PV(J) 2183
          I'm not beggin' nobody
              (alt tk)   Tpt LP 801,
DRC 216   Shuckin' mama   Tpt LP 700, ALCD 2700, PV(J) 2183

(Note: DRC 211 also mastered as ACA 3036, DRC 214-2 as ACA 3246 & 3201)

———

v/hca with Dave Campbell, p-1; B. B. King, g; J. V. Turner, g; Carl "Wimpy" Jones, g; Raz Roseby, b; Junior Blackman; d.
Jackson MS 12 Nov 1954

DRC 212-1 From the bottom-1   PV CD 2183, PV(J) 2183
DRC 212-2 From the bottom-1   -   , PV(J) 2183

DRC 212-3 From the bottom-1   Tpt 228, LP 801, PV(J) 2183
DRC 213   No nights by myself Ace 511, Teem LP 5005,
                                Trp LP 801, PV(J) 2183

(Note: DRC 212 also mastered as ACA 3037 DRC 214-2 as ACA 3043 & 3202)

BABY BOY WARREN
WITH SONNY BOY WILLIAMSON

Baby Boy Warren (Robert Henry Warren) v/g; Sonny Boy Williamson, hca; Washboard Willie, wsb
Detroit 1954

Sanafee (Not welcome anymore)	JVB 26. Exlo 2211, LP 8011, BC LP 12, Nthk LP104, Exlo PCD 2814
	Excello CD2002
Hello Stranger	Kingfish LP 1001
	Excello CD2002
Chicken [inst]	JVB 59, Drummond 3002
Chuc-a-luck (Chicken [inst])	Exlo 2211, BC LP 12 PCD 2814
	Excello CD2002
Baby boy blues (Bring my machine gun)	JVB 59, Drummond 3002. BC LP 12, **Excello CD2002**

Sonny Boy Williamson (vcl. hca) Willie "Red" Love, (p), Joe Willie Wilkins (g), "Destruction" (b) James Peck Curtis (d), Detroit 1954

Mailman, mailman	Blue(?) 2591
Pretty Little Thing	-

'Fessor Mojo's "Don't Start Me To Talkin"

> Note: Above is a public performance and probably bootlegged. Love above is no relation to Willie or Jaspar Love though he is a Memphis pianist. "Destruction" is most probably Bill Johnson of "Bill Johnson's Blue Flames" (see Junior Parker discography) as this was his nickname and indeed Matt Murphy knew no other. Blues Unlimited 8, 1964

"SONNY BOY" WILLIAMSON

v/hca withOtis Spann, p;Muddy Waters, g;Jimmy Rogers, g; Willie Dixon, b; Fred Below, d.
Chicago 12 Aug 1955

7889	Work with me	Ch LP 417
7890	Don't start me talkin'	Ckr 824, LP 1437, 1522, 50027,206, Argo, LP 4026
7891	All my love in vain	Ckr 824, LP 1427
7892	Good evening everybody	Ch LP 417
7893	You killing me (on my feet)	-

v/hca with Otis Spann, p; Robert Lockwood Jr., g; Luther Tucker, g; Willie Dixon, b; Fred Below, d.
Chicago 24 Jan 1956

7980	Let me explain	Ckr 834, LP 1437, 50027, 206
7981	I know what love is all about	Ch LP 417
7982	I wonder why	-
7983	Your imagination	Ckr 834, Ch LP 206
7984	Don't lose your eye	Ch LP 417, LP 206

Omit Otis Spann, p.
Chicago 7 Aug 1956

8205	Keep it to yourself	Ckr 847, LP 417, 206
8206	Please forgive	
	(keep it to yourself)	Ckr LP 1437
8207	The key to your door	Ckr 847, LP 1437, 206
	The key to your door [alt tk]	Ch(E) Box 1, CD 9343
8208	Have you ever been in love	Ch LP 417

Same
Chicago 8 Feb 1957

8408-2	Hurts me too much	Blues Ball LP 2004
8408-3	Hurts me too much	-
8408-5	Hurts me too much	-
8409	Fattenin' frogs for snakes	Ckr 864, LP 1437, 1528, 50027, Argo LP 4034
	Fattenin' frogs for snakes (alt tk)	Blues Ball LP 2004, Ch CD9343
8410	I don't know	Ckr 864, LP 1437
	I don't know [alt tk]	Ch CD 9330
8411	Like Wolf	Ch LP 417, 206
8412	This is my apartment	-

Add Otis Spann, p.
Chicago 1 Sept 1957

8593-1/2	Cross my heart	Ch (J) LP 6023
8593-3	Cross my heart	- , Ch (E) Box 1
8593	Cross my heart	Ckr 910, LP 1437, 50027, 206
8594	Born blind	Ckr 883, Ch LP 417, 206

8595-1	99	Ch(J) LP 6023, Ch(E) Box 1
8595-2/3	"99"	Ch LP 206
8595	Ninety nine	Ckr 883, LP 1437, 50027
8596-1/3	Dissatisfied	Ch(J) LP 6023, Ch(E) Box 1
8596	Dissatisfied	Ckr 910, LP 1427, 1503

—

Same session

18030	Little village [takes 1 to 11]	Ch LP 1536
18030-1	Little village	Ch LP 2-92519, Ch(E) Box 1
18031	Unseen eye	Ch LP 1536

(Note: Dialogue omitted from 18030 on Chess LP 92519)

—

v/hca with Lafayette Leake, p; Robert Lockwood Jr., g; Eugene Pierson, g, Willie Dixon, b; Fred Below, d.
Chicago 27 Mar 1958

8753-2/4	Your funeral and my trial	Ch(J) LP 6023
8753-5	Your funeral and my trial	- , Ch(E) Box 1
8753	Your funeral and my trial	Ckr 894, LP 1437, 1528, 50027
8754	She got next to me	Ch LP 1536
	She got next to me [alt tk]	Ch LP 206
8755-2	Wake up baby	Ch(J) LP 6023, CD 9324
8755	Wake up baby	Ckr 894, LP1437, 50027
8756	Keep your hands out of my pocket	Ch LP 1536, 206

—

v/hca with Harold Burrage p-1, Willie Dixon, b.
Chicago 1958

Steady rollin' man	Flyr(E) 567, Paula CD 07
Take your hands out of my pocket	- , -

(Note: Cobra recordings)

CHARLES CLARK AND WILLIE DIXON BAND WITH SONNY BOY WILLIAMSON

Charles Clark, v; Sonny Boy Williamson, hca; Harold Burrage, p; Otis Rush, Louis Myers, g; Willie Dixon, b; Billie Stepney, d.
Chicago 1958

	Row your boat	Flyr LP 594
	Row your boat	Flyr LP 567
	Row your boat	-
C-1040	Row your boat	Artistic 1500, Paula PCD-7
C-1041	Hidden charms	-

---

v/hca with Otis Spann, p; Robert Lockwood Jr., g; Luther Tucker, g; Willie Dixon, b; Odie Payne, d.
Chicago 1958

9479	Let your conscience be your guide	Ckr 927, Ch LP 417, 206
9480	Unseeing eye	- , - , -

Fred Below, d. replaces Payne
Chicago 30 Jan 1960

9829-1	The goat	Ch(J) LP 6023
	The goat [band track]	- , CD 9340
9829	The goat	Ckr 943, Ch LP 1509
9830-1	Cool disposition	Ch(J) 6023, Ch(E) Box 1
9830-3	Cool disposition	- , -
	Cool disposition	Ch LP 417
9831	I never do wrong	Ch LP 206
9832	It's sad to be alone	Ckr 943, Ch LP 1503, 1522, 50027, 206

v/hca with Otis Spann, p; Robert Lockwood Jr., g; Luther Tucker, g, Fred Below, d.
Chicago 14 Apr 1960

10105	Open road	Ch LP 1536
10106	Santa Claus	- , 206
10107	I can't do it without you	-
10108	Checkin' up on my baby	Ch LP 1503, 50027
	Checkin' up on my baby [alt tk]	Ch(E) Box 1

v/hca with Otis Spann, p; Eddie King, g; Luther Tucker, g; Willie Dixon, b, Fred Below, d.
Chicago Jun 1960

10266	Temperature 110	Chr 956, Ch LP 1536
10267	Peach tree	Ch LP 1503
10268	Lonesome cabin	Ckr 956, Ch LP 1536
10269	Somebody help me	Ch LP 1509

v/hca with Lafayette Leake, p; Robert Lockwood Jr, g; Luther Tucker, g, Willie Dixon, v-1/b
Chicago 15 Sep 1960

10415	Down child	Ckr 1134, Ch LP 1503, 50027
10416	Trust my baby	Ckr 963, Ch LP 1503, 50027
10417	This old life	Ch LP 1536
10418	Too close together - 1	Ckr 963, Ch LP 417, 206

v/hca with Otis Spann, p; Robert Lockwood Jr., g; Luther Tucker, g; Willie Dixon, v-1/b, Odie Payne, d.
Chicago 14 Dec 1960

10569	Too young to die	Ch LP 1503, 50027
10570	She's my baby	Ch LP 1509
10571	Stop right now	Ckr 975, Ch LP 1509
10572	The hunt - 1	- , -

Fred Below, d, replaces Payne
Chicago 8 Sep 1961

11224	Too old to drink (think)	Ch LP 1503
11225	That's all I want	-
11226-1/4	One way out	Ch(J) LP 6023
11226	One way out	Ckr 1003, Ch LP 417
11227-1/3	Nine below zero	Ch(J) LP 6023, Ch(E) Box 1
11227	Nine below zero	Ch LP 206
11227	Nine below zero	Ckr 1003, Ch LP 1509, 50027

JOSH WHITE W/SONNY BOY WILLIAMSON

Josh White, v/g; Sonny Boy Williamson, hca, Floyd Morris, p; Herb Brown, b; Eddie Williams, d, unk, 2nd vcl.
Chicago 4 Jan 1963

26876	Blues came from Texas	Merc LP 20724
26877	Hard-headed woman	Merc LP 20861
26878	In the evening	Merc LP 20724
26879	Evil-hearted woman	-
26886	Goin' down slow	Merc LP 20821
26887	How long	-
26888	'lijah -1	Merc LP 20724
26889	Howling wolf	-
26890	Lula	Merc LP 20821
26891	You don't know my mind	-
26892	Death comin' back	-
26895	Hoe boys	Merc LP 20724
26896	Tamp 'em up solid	Merc LP 20821

'Fessor Mojo's "Don't Start Me To Talkin"

v/hca with Lafayette Leake or Billy Emerson, org; Matt Murphy, g, Milton Rector Jr., b; Al Duncan, d.
Chicago 11 Jan 1963

12113	Got to move	Ch LP 1503, 50027, 206
12114	Bye bye bird	Ckr 1036, Ch LP 1509
12115	Help me	- , - , 50027, 206
12116	Bring it on home	Ckr 1134, Ch LP 1503, 1533, 500227, 206, Argo LP 4031

v/hca with Jarrett Gibson, Donald Hankins, saxes; Lafayette Leake, p; Buddy Guy,, g; Jack Meyers, b; Clifton James, d.
Chicago 3 Sept 1963

12663	One way out	Ch(E) Box 1
12664	My younger days	Ckr 1080, Ch LP 1509, 50027
12665	Trying to get back on my feet	Ckr 1065, -
12666	Decoration day	- , -

Otis Spann

v/piano with Sonny Boy Williamson, hca; J. T. Brown, ts; Matt Murphy, g; Willie Dixon, b, Billie Stepney, d
Chicago, IL 21 Sep 1963

Skies are blue	Ckr unissued
My baby is gone	-
Love is a miracle	-
No, no, no	-

v/hca
Baden-Baden (G) 27 Sep 1963

I'm layin' down and thinking	Document (Au) 575
I have a right to trust my baby	-
Bye bye blues	-
Blues of the blues	-
Work with me	-
I'm the loneliest man	-

VICTORIA SPIVEY WITH SONNY BOY WILLIAMSON

v/uke, Sonny Boy Williamson, hca; Gunter Boas, p.
28 Sept 1963

156	Careless love	unissued
157	St. Louis blues -1	-
158	Black snake swinger -1	Spivey LP 1012

v/hca with Otis Spann, p/v-2; Matt Murphy, g; Willie Dixon, b; Billie Stepney, V/hca only -1, hca/only -3
Bremen (G) 13 Oct 1963

Sonny Boy's harmonica boogie - 1	Fon(G) LP 681, 510, Fon(E) LP5204
Walkin' in my father's track - 1	unissued
I don't know (why she disappoints me so)	Fon(G) LP 681, 510, Fon(E) LP5204
Blues Ball	LP 2004, ECD 26071-2
A lonely man	unissued

'Fessor Mojo's "Don't Start Me To Talkin"

Bye bye bird - 1	Scout (G) LP 1
In my own words - 1	-
Had my fun	ECD 26071-2

From Above

That's all I want baby	FCD 26100
Your love for me is true	ACT(G) 9205-2
Don't misuse me	- , FCD 26100
I'm gettin' tired -1	- , FCD 26100
Goin' Down Slow	FCD 26100
Sonny Boy's harmonica blues -3	FCD 26100, ECD 26071-2

Same

99-1	Red Lightnin' RL(E) Lp 0060
Bye bye bird -1	-
All my love in vain	-
Your funeral and my trial	-
Don't start me to talking	-

Same

Bye bye bird -1	Rarity(E) LP 1
So sad to be lonesome	-
Nine below zero	-
Don't tell nobody else	-
Just a dirty story (speech)	-

ROLAND KIRK
WITH SONNY BOY WILLIAMSON

Roland Kirk, ts, mn, str, fl; "Big Skol" (Sonny Boy Williamson), hca; Tete Montoliu, p; Neils Orsted Pederson, Don Moore , b; J. C. Moses,d.
Oct 1963 Copenhagen (Dk)

Blues	Roland Kirk Box Set
The Monkey Thing	Roland Kirk Box Set

v/hca with Memphis Slim, v-1,p-2; Matt Murphy, g-3, Billie Stepney, d-4.
Copenhagen(Dk) 1 Nov 1963

Don't let your right hand	Sv(Dk) LP 158, Alligator CD 4787
I can't understand	Sv(Dk) LP 158, Alligator CD 4787
Movin' down the river Rhine	Sv(Dk) LP 170, -
When the lights went out	Sv(Dk) LP 170, Alligator CD 4787
The sky is crying - 3	Sv(Dk) LP 158, Sv(Dk) STCD 8012
Coming home to your baby -1	- , -
Gettin' together - 3	- , -
Slowly walk close to me -1	- , -
Why are you crying - 3	Sv(Dk) LP 170 , -
Once upon a time - 3	- , -
Down and out - 3	SV(Dk) EP 415, Sv(Dk) STCD 8012
Down and out -3	SV(Dk) LP 222 , -
I wonder do I have a friend -2	SV(Dk) LP 158 , -
Sonny Boy's girlfriend -2	SV(Dk) LP 170, Alligator CD 4787
Same girl - 1,2	- . -
Little girl - 2,3,4	SV(Dk) LP 158, Sv(Dk) STCD 8012
I'm so glad - 2,3,4	SV(Dk) LP 170 , -
Movin on - 2,3,4	SV(Dk) LP 170, Alligator CD 4787
Tippin though customs - 2.3.4	SV(Dk) CD 8012,
The Story of Sonny Boy Williamson -3.4	
	SV(Dk) LP 158, Sv(Dk) STCD 8012
On my way back home - 3.4	SV(Dk) LP 170 , -
Rebecca blues - 1	SV(Dk) LP 168 , -

'Fessor Mojo's "Don't Start Me To Talkin"

> Released as **Memphis Slim** p, with Sonny Boy Williamson, hca, Matt Murphy g-2
>
> Early one morning   Sv(Dk) EP 415, LP 222
> Copenhagen woman-2   Sv(Dk) LP 188

—

v/hca/g-1 with Erik Host, g; (except -1), vocal only -2
Copenhagen (Dk) 5 Nov 1963

CS-1	Baby, let me come back home (Baby please come back home)	Collectors Special(Dk) EP 101
CS-2	November boogie [inst]	-
CS-3	All night boogie [inst]	-
CS-4	Leavin' blues	-
CS-5	Kind hearted woman - 1	Rarity(E) LP 1
CS-6	Milky white way - 2	-

—

v/hca with Lennart Nylen, g; Sture Nordin, b; v\hca only -1
Copenhagen (Dk) November 1963

Who's gonna take care of you   Sv (Dk) 8012
It's raining outdoors, baby   -
Have you enjoyed my play -1   -

(Note: The above derives from a film soundtrack.)

—

SONNY BOY WILLIAMSON & MEMPHIS SLIM

v/hca with Memphis Slim, p-1, unk p-2; b-3
"Live at Blue Bar, Paris (F) 1 Dec 1963

The skies are crying -1,-3	Vg(F) LP 639-30, 410	
Your funeral and my trial, -2	- , -	
Explain yourself to me, -2	- , -	
Nine below zero, -1, -3	- , -	
Fattenin' Frogs for snakes, -1	- , -	
My one room cabin	- , -	
Gettin' out of town	- , -	

(Issued in the US as GNP-Crescendo LP 10003.)

—

SONNY BOY WILLIAMSON & THE YARDBIRDS

v/hca with Eric Clapton, Chris Dreja, g; Paul Samwell-Smith, b; Jim McCarty, b, v/hca only -1
Live at the Crawdaddy Club, Richmond, Surrey (E) 8 Dec 1963

37575	Bye bye bird -1	Fon (E) LP 5277, OPCD 0125, ECD 26071-2
37576	Mister Downchild	- , - , -
37577	23 hours too long	- , - , -
37578	Out on the Water Coast	- , - , -
37579	Baby don't worry -1	-
37580	Pontiac blues	- , OPCD 0125, ECD 26071-2
37581	Take it easy baby	- , - , - , (two versions)
37582	I don't care no more -1	- , - , -
37583	Do the Weston [inst]	- ECD 26071-2
	The River Rhine	L+R (G) LP 42.020, OPCD 0125
	A lost care	- , -
	Western Arizona	- , -
	Honey on your hips	OPCD 0125

(Note: Fontana(E) LP 5277 reissued in stereo on LP 960, and issued in the US on Mercury LP 21071 & 61071. Matrixes allocated by Mercury. "Western Arizona" is identical to "Do the Weston" minus the middle guitar break.)

Ottilie Patterson with Sonny Boy Williamson
v; Ottilie Patterson; Sonny Boy Williamson hca, unk g, b, d, org. arr. by Ivor Raymonds
London 23 Dec 1963

Baby Please Don't Go	Columbia (UK) 7208
I Feel So Good	Columbia (UK) 7208

—

SONNY BOY WILLIAMSON & THE ANIMALS

v/hca with Eric Burdon, v-1; Alan Price, org/p; Hilton Valentine, g; Chas Chandler, b; John Steel, d.
Live at Club a Go Go, Newcastle-upon-Tyne (E) 30 Dec 1963

Sonny's slow walk	Charly(E) LP 30199, OPCD 0125
Pontiac blues	- , -
My babe	- ,
I don't care no more	- ,
Baby, don't you worry	- ,
Night time is the right time -1	- ,
I'm gonna put you down	- ,
Fattenin' frogs for snakes	- ,
Nobody but you -1	- ,
Bye bye Sonny bye bye (Coda) -1 -	,
Bye bye Burdon	OPCD 0125

(Note: Reissued on Charly CD-25 and in the U. S. on Springboard LP 4065.)

SONNY BOY WILLIAMSON and CHRIS BARBER'S JAZZ BAND

v/hca with Pat Halcox, tp; Chris Barber, tb/b; Ian Wheeler, cl; Eddie Smith, bj; Dick Smith, b; Graham, d.
London (E) 1 Jan 1964

Pontiac blues	unissued private recording
Sonny boy's slow walk	-
C jam blues (inst)	-
Harmonica and bass blues/ West Memphis	-

SONNY BOY WILLIAMSON & THE YARDBIRDS

v/hca with Eric Clapton, Chris Dreja, g; Paul Samwell-Smith, b; Jim McCarty, b, v/hca only -1
Live at Town Hall, Birmingham (E) 28 Feb 1964

Slow walk	Byg (F) LP 529,705,Charly CDLK80
Highway 61 (Pontiac blues)	- , -
My little cabin (lonesome cabin)	- , -
Bye bye bird -1	- , -

(Reissued on Decal (E) LP 54 and Charly CD 80.)

v/hca; Jarrett Gibson, Donald Hankins, saxes, Buddy Guy, g; Jack Myers, b, Fred Below, d.
Chicago 30 April 1964

13210	Stop Cryin'	Ch(E) Box 1, Ch LP 206
13211	(I want you) Close to Me	Ckr 1080, Ch LP 1509
13212	One Way Out	- , Ch LP 1503, 50027, 206

'Fessor Mojo's "Don't Start Me To Talkin"

> (Note: 13209 Issued under Buddy Guy's name)
>
> 13209   I Dig Your Wig (edited)-1   Ch 1899, Blues Ball LP 2005
> 13209   I Dig Your Wig-1   Ch CD 2-9337

SONNY BOY WILLIAMSON and THE CHRIS BARBER BAND

v/hca with Pat Halcox, tp; Chris Barber, tb/b; Ian Wheeler, cl; Eddie Smith, bj; Dick Smith, b; Graham Burbidge, d, v/hca only -1; Ottilie Patterson, 2nd v; -2. .

Live Free Trade Hall in Manchester (E) 31 May 1964

Help me	BL (E) LP 12126/7
C Jam Blues {inst]	unissued
So sad to be lonesome	-
Walk with me baby	BL (E) LP 12126/7
Bye bye bird (Bird, I'm goin')	unissued
Your funeral, my trial -1	-
Pontiac blues & encore	BL (E) LP 12126/7
When the Saints go marchin' in	unissued
This little light of mine	-
Saints [inst reprise]	-

v/hca with Jarrett Gibson, Donald Hankins, saxes (except -1), Lafayette Leake, org -2,p-3, Buddy Guy, g; (except 1), unk, b; d.

Chicago August 1964

	I can't be alone -3	Ch LP 206
15172-1	Don't make a mistake (Mattie is my wife)	
		Blues Ball 2004, Blue Night 1668
15172-2	Don't make a mistake (Mattie is my wife)	
		Blues Ball 2004, Blue Night 1668

15173	Understand my life	Ch LP 206
15174	Find another woman -1	Blues Ball 2004, Blue Night 1668
	My name is Sonny Boy Williamson	Blue Night 1668

(Note: 15172-1/2 also given as 15172-3/4.)

---

v/hca with Sunnyland Slim, p; Hubert Sumlin, g.
Hamburg (G) 9 Oct 1964

Dissatisfied	Font (E) LP 5225, Scout (G) LP 1
	FCD 26100

---

v/hca with Hubert Sumlin, g.
Munich (G) 12 Oct 1964

I'm trying to make London my home	Font (E) LP 5225, FCD 26100, ECD 26071-2
I got to cut out	ACT(G) 9204-2, FCD 26100

---

v/hca with Joe Harriott, as; Alan Skidmore, ts; Brian Auger, org; Jimmy Page, g, Ricky Brown, b, Mick Waller, d.
London Apr 1965

Don't send me no flowers	Marmalade (E) LP 607004
I see a man downstairs (one way out)	-
She was dumb	-
The goat	-
Walking	-
Little girl how old are you	-
It's a bloody life	-
Getting out of town	-

(Note: LP 607004 reissued on Charly (E) CD LK 80)

v/hca with Houston Stackhouse, g; and Peck Curtis, d.
Helena AK May 1965

King Biscuit theme	Arh EP 530, CD 310	
V-8 Ford blues	- ,	-
Stormy Monday	- ,	-
Right now	- ,	-
Come go with me	- ,	-

(Note: The above is a complete broadcast of the KFFA radio show "King Biscuit Time" including commercials and announcements. See Also Memphis Slim.)

—

Sources: Blues Records 1943-1970, Volume One (1987), Leadbitter & Slaven Volume Two (1994), Leadbitter, Fancourt & Pelletier, Record Information Services, London England and Various CD liner notes

---

**Send Corrections, Expansions & Updates to William E. Donoghue
RFCW94A@Prodigy.com or
sonnyboy@donoghue.com**

Who is 'Fessor Mojo?

William E. Donoghue, author of "Don't Start Me Talkin", has had a lifetime love affair with jazz and blues music. In his teens he enjoyed early rock and roll, jump blues and Doo-Wop from the front row of the Uptown Theater in Philadelphia. Later he was active in the Philadelphia Folk Festival, enjoyed many jazz matinees at Pep's and the Showboat and watch the Summer of Love come east to The Electric Factory in Philadelphia.

He is currently developing "Don't Start Me Talkin", the extensive and authoritative video documentary on Sonny Boy Williamson II. He is on the board of advisors of BluesAid, a charity of the Sonny Boy Blues Society.

In his day job, he is an financial educator, editor of a newsletter and a successful author with over a million books in print.

Physically he resides in Seattle WA but his heart is in the Mississippi Delta.

'Fessor Mojo's "Don't Start Me To Talkin"

ORDER FORM

Qty.	Title	Price	Can. Price	Total
	Collectors' Edition 'Fessor Mojo	$19.95	$24.95	
	Shipping & Handling (add $3.00 for one book, $2.00 for each additional book)			
	Sales Tax (WA Residents only, add 8.2%)			
	Total enclosed			

Telephone Orders:
Call (800) 982-2455
Have your VISA or MasterCard ready.

Fax Orders:
(206) 281-1625
Fill out order blank and fax.

Postal Orders:
Mojo Visions
P.O. Box 19535
Seattle, WA 98109

Payment: Please Check One

☐ **Check**

☐ **VISA**

☐ **MasterCard**

Expiration Date: _____ / _____
Card #: _____
Name on Card: _____

Name _____
Address _____
City _____ **State** _____ **Zip** _____
Daytime Phone (___) _____

Quantity discounts are available.
For more information, call (206) 281-1516 ext. 207.

Thank you for your order!

I understand that I may return any books for a full refund if not satisfied

'Fessor Mojo's "Don't Start Me To Talkin"